MW00559870

How to Start and Operate a

Profitable Tour Business

Make Money While Traveling and Guiding Tours;

a perfect business for the early retiree!

Gordon R Bartlett

June, 2014

A common sense, step-by-step guide written by a man who, in 1993, started a tour business in a remote Arizona city and operated it profitably for 19 years.

ISBN 978-0-692-26675-5

Group Tour Solutions
4065 Northstar Drive
Lake Havasu City, Arizona 86406

Email: gbartlet@citlink.net

Disclaimer

Gordon and Patty Bartlett

Table of Contents

INTRODUCTION 1

   BACKGROUND 1

   ABOUT THE AUTHOR 4

      The Early Years 4

      Corporate Career 5

      Retirement from IBM 6

      Why Start a Tour Business? 7

      A Personal Need to be Productive and Earn Money! 8

   ABOUT LAKE HAVASU CITY, ARIZONA 9

WHO CAN BENEFIT FROM READING THIS BOOK? 13

THE BASICS OF THE TOUR BUSINESS 15

   DEFINITIONS 15

      What is a Tour Operator? 15

      What is a Group Tour Operator? 16

      What is a Tour Director or Tour Manager? 17

      What is a Step-On Guide? 17

      What is a Driver-Narrator? 18

      What is a Receptive Operator? 18

      What is a Pre-Formed Group? 19

INGREDIENTS FOR THE SUCCESS OF A TOUR OPERATOR 21

      1) A Strong Personality and Good Speaking Ability 21

      2) Good Destination Possibilities 22

      3) A Business Plan 22

      4) Desire and Determination 23

      5) Customer Base 24

      6) Internet/Web Site 24

      7) Advertising and Marketing 25

      8) Excellent Customer Service 26

      9) Employees 26

      10) Customer Records 27

      11) Accounting/Finance 27

      12) Insurance and Legal Protection 28

ANALYZING YOUR MARKET 31

THE 15 STEPS TO YOUR FIRST TOUR 35

IDENTIFYING TOUR POSSIBILITIES 39

   POSSIBILITIES FOR SHORT TOURS: 39

PREPARING A PRELIMINARY TOUR ITINERARY 41

   USING A COMPUTER MAPPING PROGRAM 41

INCLUDING MEALS WHILE ON TOUR 44

SAMPLE PRICES OF TOURS 45

SCOUTING YOUR TOURS 47

RESTROOM STOPS 47

FINDING INTERESTING STOPS ALONG THE WAY 48

EVALUATING HOTELS AND MOTELS 52

KEEP TRACK OF SCOUTING EXPENSES 56

KEEP GOOD NOTES ON YOUR SCOUTING TRIP 57

HOW TO CHARTER A BUS 59

WHY YOU SHOULD NEVER OWN A BUS 59

SELECTING A CHARTER BUS COMPANY 61

CALCULATING THE PRICE FOR A TOUR 65

USING A SPREADSHEET PROGRAM 65

PRICING TO MAKE A PROFIT 68

PROFIT FROM A MAJOR TOUR OR CRUISE 70

GETTING QUOTES FOR HOTELS & MOTELS 71

ADVERTISING AND PROMOTING YOUR TOURS 73

THE IMPORTANCE OF A LOGO 74

NEWSPAPER ADVERTISING 76

ADS IN LOCAL LIVE THEATRE PROGRAMS 77

A TOUR BROCHURE 78

PRODUCING AND MAILING A TOUR BROCHURE 80

A WEBSITE FOR YOUR TOUR BUSINESS 82

LOCAL PROMOTION OPPORTUNITIES 84

CONDUCTING YOUR OWN TOURS 87

PREPARING FOR YOUR TOUR 87

Confirming Details of the Tour to Your Travelers 87

Information Forms 88

Terms and Conditions 89

Dealing with Disruptive Travelers 89

Meal Selections 91

Handling Final Payments 92

Badges, Luggage Tags & Boarding Passes 92

THE GROUP MEETING PLACE 94

MANAGEMENT DETAILS WHILE ON THE BUS 100

Getting Everyone Acquainted 102

Commentary While Traveling 104

Getting On and Off the Bus 105

Water and Snacks While Traveling 106

Rotating Seats on the Bus 107

Arrival at your Hotel 108

MUSIC AND VIDEOS ON THE BUS 109

FREQUENT TRAVELER AWARDS 111

SELLING YOUR FUTURE TOURS WHILE ON THE BUS 112

At the End of the Tour 113

Teaming Up with your Bus Driver 114

    Tipping the Driver on a Tour...*115*

    Tipping the Driver on a Transfer...*117*

EXPANDING THE DISTANCE AND LENGTH OF YOUR TOURS.........**119**

Contracting with a Large Tour Company 121

Using a City Sightseeing Company 127

Escorting Groups through Airports 129

    Airport Check-In..*130*

    Using Kiosks to Check In..*132*

OFFERING OCEAN CRUISES...**133**

Dealing with Cruise Lines 133

Getting your Group to the Pier 137

Arriving at the Pier 139

Your Work, Once On-Board the Ship 142

OFFERING OVERNIGHT RIVER CRUISES **145**

The Details of Booking a River Cruise 147

COMPARING OCEAN AND RIVER CRUISES...............................**151**

ESCORTING A MAJOR TOUR **155**

OFFERING TRAVEL INSURANCE **159**

SETTING UP OFFICE PROCEDURES **165**

The Need for a Computer 165

    Internet *166*

    Email..*167*

    Word Processing...*167*

    Spreadsheets...*167*

    Publishing..*168*

    Accounting...*169*

    Customer Records...*171*

    Mapping...*176*

RUNNING YOUR OFFICE **177**

KEEPING UP WITH THE TOUR INDUSTRY **181**

Tour Magazines 181

Tour Associations 182

Trade Shows and "Fam" Tours 183

CONCLUSION **187**

ILLUSTRATIONS **189**

Introduction

Background

On May 15, 2012, I sold Bartlett Tours, Inc., the business my wife, Patty, and I had operated for 19 years in Lake Havasu City, Arizona. As the sale progressed and I found myself coaching and writing procedures for the new owner over a several month period, I became convinced that other people could start a tour business too, if only they had a guide to follow. I hope you find this book a helpful guide to your success in your own tour business!

We started our business in Lake Havasu City in 1993 after moving from Tucson, Arizona. The population of Lake Havasu City was about 22,000. We were 20 miles from the closest freeway, Interstate 40, and we were 150 miles from the closest commercial airport in Las Vegas. So, Lake Havasu City would certainly be described by most people as "remote".

We were "unknowns" in town so getting started was a challenge. We did some advertising in the local newspaper and offered a 5-day tour of Southern Arizona, a region that we knew well from living there for twenty years and from our own travels. We even rented a meeting room at a local hotel and offered refreshments to those who would come to hear and see a slide presentation about our first tour offering.

To our dismay, not one person showed up to our meeting. We had plenty of punch and cookies for the two of us. Patty said maybe we should give up the idea of starting a tour company. But, I was not interested in giving up, because I could see the potential.

I explained to Patty that starting a tour business was a reasonably low financial risk. We didn't need a "real" office because we could work from our home; we didn't need to buy inventory, we didn't need to buy a bus, we didn't need to hire employees and the best thing is that it is customary in the tour business to collect final payments at least 30 days before the tour departs.

We decided that maybe the 5-day "Southern Arizona Circle Tour" was too long and too expensive for some unknown tour operators to try as their first tour. Instead, we began advertising a couple of two and three-day tours and the phone began to ring.

Just one or two calls a day got us excited. A few people began to sign up and send us a deposit. However, we were hoping to get 30 to 40 people so that we could charter a nice new bus for the trip. "Charter" is the term for renting a bus with a licensed, experienced driver. Instead, 30 days before the tour we had <u>just nine people</u>.

Rather than cancel due to an insufficient number of participants, I looked into renting a 15-passenger van from a local rental agency. I first checked with the Arizona Motor Vehicle Department to make sure it was legal to drive paying passengers without a commercial driver's license.

I found that in Arizona and in most states, it is perfectly legal to drive paying passengers with a regular driver's license as long as there are 15 or fewer passengers. Our first tour left in May, 1993 with nine passengers and high expectations.

We visited the former mining town of Jerome, Arizona; toured beautiful red-rock country in Sedona and went on a scenic train ride along the Verde River near Cottonwood. At the end of this tour, our first travelers were very excited to hear what other tours we were planning. I asked each one to spread the word by telling their friends about Bartlett Tours.

We continued to rent vans for our next four tours in 1993 with passenger numbers ranging from 11 to just 3. But, our phone was ringing; the word was getting around!

After some local advertising, for our sixth tour, in December 1993 to the Glory of Christmas pageant at the Crystal Cathedral in Orange County, California, we had 46 people. For the first time, we could charter a bus (I'll call it a "bus" in this book, but this type of luxury vehicle is often called a "motorcoach").

I'm pleased to say, that the perseverance paid off because we never had to go back to using a van. Over the next 19 years until we sold our business in May 2012, we completed a total of 171 tours and cruises and averaged a passenger count of 44. All of this was done without an employee, office (other than in our home) or bus.

With the information provided in this book, and your own determination, you can do this too.

Sometime in early 2011, I was approached by a friend and fellow member of a local leads organization, The Referrals Club, who said to me, "If you're ever thinking about selling your tour business, I'd like to talk to you". My response was that it was probably about a year away, but, "let's talk".

I'm happy to report that the new owners, Mike and Leeann, have completed twenty-two tours in the 24 months since acquiring Bartlett Tours in May, 2012. The response from our regular travelers has been great!

Mike and Leeann asked to purchase the "Bartlett Tours" name because we had established a very good reputation and the name was well known in our town.

Mike and Leeann have established themselves as professionals who have their travelers' best interests at heart. Patty and I are very pleased with the positive continuation of the business that we began and put our heart into for 19 years.

About the Author

The Early Years

I was born Gordon Robert Bartlett on July 25, 1938 in Pomona, California. My father was a citrus grower, raising oranges and lemons under the Sunkist cooperative label. My mother was a traditional homemaker. I was raised on a 30-acre orange and lemon grove and loved to play outdoors.

I had an older brother, a cat, a dog and a donkey and life was good! I went to school in Claremont, California from kindergarten through my 12th grade. I was class president several times through the years and was student body president in my senior year (1955-1956) at Claremont High School. There were just 81 in my graduating class and we continue to enjoy class reunions every few years.

At a young age I had an interest in business. Even when I had a dozen chickens laying eggs, I would record each day the number of eggs produced and my revenue from selling the extras to neighbors. I also picked up ripe lemons that had dropped from our trees and sold them for fifteen cents a dozen from a small stand on the road running by our home. Remember, folks didn't have frozen lemonade concentrate in the forties and fifties.

I tried a year of college, worked for nearly a year for a telephone company collecting coin boxes from pay phones, and then, in 1958, volunteered for the draft to get my military service out of the way. After serving two years in the Army I returned home to finish college and graduated with a degree in Business Administration from California State Polytechnic College (Cal Poly) in Pomona, California.

Patty and I were married while I was in college and I joined IBM three days after graduating in March, 1963. After three months of training in one of the Los Angeles offices and in Lexington, Kentucky, I began as a Marketing Rep in Los

Angeles County in the Accounting Machine Department of the Electric Typewriter Division. We had two products to sell in various configurations that competed with ledger posting machines made by NCR and Burroughs. In 1965 I transferred to Riverside, California and joined the sales team for the Data Processing Division of IBM, selling punched card data processing machines.

Corporate Career

My career with International Business Machines (IBM) spanned 28 years and 3 months, first in Southern California and then the last twenty years in Tucson, Arizona. During most of that time, I was a marketing rep involved in the sale of data processing equipment to local customers both large and small.

I held the position of marketing manager at two different times in my career with about twelve people in my unit each time. But, in 1968 and early 1969 I held a position in IBM's Western Region Promotional Services Department in Los Angeles. Here I worked for Art Kane, who was responsible for Western Region sales and systems engineering recognition events, major management meetings, producing brochures for our region and making movies for use in the western 13 states.

Art was a stickler for detail because we only had "one chance to do it right". When we got within a month of producing a major event, he put up a poster in our office that read, "When you're absolutely certain, check one more time". This training and experience under Art Kane served me very well in the rest of my IBM career but was even more important in designing and planning 171 tours and cruises with real people who had paid good money for the experience.

The tour business is a business with many details that all need to be verified and confirmed to make sure the travelers come away from their tour wanting more of the same.

Although I was very happy and successful during my years in Tucson as Senior Marketing Representative, after some intense "pushing", in 1988 I took on the position of Marketing Manager in Tucson. I was very fortunate to have had about a dozen highly motivated younger people work for me in both sales and systems engineering positions.

My work as marketing manager in Tucson lasted three and a half years, until IBM announced an early retirement offer in March, 1991 that I could not refuse. Fortunately, the forty-two months spent as a marketing manager were the most lucrative of my career and thus were a positive influence on my retirement earnings.

Retirement from IBM

IBM offered an "early out" in 1991 to all employees who had more than 25 years with the company. At the time, I had over 28 years of service, and although I had a very satisfying career, I was ready to do something else.

At the time I retired, I was just short of 53 years of age, so total retirement was not of interest to me. During the last 13 years prior to retirement, I had purchased single-family homes in Tucson and operated them as rentals. At the time of my retirement from IBM, I had 14 single-family houses, a small eight-unit trailer park and 40 acres of land in the foothills southeast of Tucson.

For the most part, I enjoyed owning these properties and the work that went along with them because, in a way, I was experiencing the good and bad of owning a business. Unlike working for a large corporation, here I made all the decisions and lived with the consequences. I did the majority of the repairs and maintenance on the rentals on nights and weekends.

When I spent a Saturday cleaning and painting a rental house, I could stand back and enjoy immediate satisfaction with my work. This is something many people experience only rarely in their corporate jobs. The properties turned out to be a very good investment over time.

After we moved from Tucson to Parker, Arizona and then to Lake Havasu City in early 1993, I sold a number of the houses to tenants who had been prompt with their rent payments and then sold the others one at a time over the next few years when a tenant moved out.

In all cases, I sold the properties with owner financing. In other words, I carried the financing and made it possible for a buyer with some past credit problems to buy a house without trying to qualify for a new real estate loan. All of the houses I bought from 1977 to 1983 had existing FHA or VA loans that were fully assumable, so, when I sold them, I utilized a legal "wrap-around" mortgage.

This meant that I could carry back financing on these properties even though the original mortgage was not paid in full. This is called a "wrap-around" mortgage and, through unfortunate changes in financing laws in 1986, is no longer possible to do. The existing FHA or VA mortgage was paid first each month through an escrow company and we were paid what was left.

The experience of owning rental properties and dealing with tenants for over 15 years, gave me the confidence that I could own and operate other types of businesses.

Why Start a Tour Business?

My wife, Patty, had helped her best friend Anne in Tucson start a Senior Citizens Center at the Amphitheatre School District in about 1985. This was an "outreach" effort to have local seniors feel more a part of the school system. The program was started by inviting near-by residents to come to the district offices where they had a large room available to host speakers, enjoy crafting and take part in other activities.

ACES, as it became known, had meetings Tuesday and Thursday from 10:00AM to 2:00PM, with a low-cost lunch included. After a few years of these activities, they began borrowing vans from the school district and taking the seniors to a park, to a movie, or to some other local activity. About this time, the Pima County Parks and Recreation Department joined the school district in sponsoring this program.

After some time of doing short day-trips, Anne and Patty decided to offer tours to places in Arizona, California, Colorado, and beyond. In most cases, the tours were done by utilizing two school vans which they each drove with about ten passengers per van. If they had enough response, they would take a third van with a county parks employee driving.

Patty and Anne scouted these tours before taking a group. Patty loved scouting and escorting these tours and would come home on a real "high". I began saying, "maybe this is what we should do when I retire from IBM".

Patty and I have always enjoyed traveling and so the tour business seemed perfect for us. It not only offered the chance to make money while taking a group on a tour but it also offered the chance of traveling by ourselves when we were "scouting" a new tour. The expenses of a scouting trip are deductible expenses against your business profits.

Our initial vision of our tour business was quite narrow. Because of our inexperience, we thought we would be doing tours of the southwest and west, but didn't see the possibility of going further. It was a pleasant surprise when, within a few years, we were planning and escorting tours and cruises around the world.

A Personal Need to be Productive and Earn Money!

I had just retired from IBM with most of my time spent as a commissioned salesman or sales manager. When your earnings are based on a commission, you get used to being self-motivated. I only earned money if I made something happen. Like the owner of a business, I had to make contacts and make sales. I had developed a habit of working smart and hard. Money earned is a way of keeping score.

The planning for Bartlett Tours began in 1992 while we were living in Parker. I only knew one person at that time that operated a tour business. Ray Manley of Ray Manley Tours in Tucson was a long-time member of my Tucson Rotary Club and had a very successful tour business.

I called Ray one day when we were planning a trip back to Tucson and he was gracious enough to meet Patty and me for lunch. Ray was a professional photographer with many of his images in Arizona featured in the high quality *Arizona Highways* magazine. We talked for over two hours about the tour business and Patty and I became even more excited about our venture.

I began designing and pricing our first tour by making a lot of phone calls to hotels, restaurants and attractions. The convenience of the Internet was not a factor in those days. As was stated above, our first tour, the "Arizona Circle Tour" never got off the ground, but we gained some good experience from our effort.

About Lake Havasu City, Arizona

We moved to Lake Havasu City in February, 1993. Our city is quite new, having been founded in 1964 by Robert McCulloch, the inventor of the lightweight chain saw. Mr. McCulloch also manufactured outboard engines at the time and in the late 1950's was looking for a suitable water site to test his engines.

Flying over Arizona, he spotted a large desert lake with a WWII vintage airstrip nearby. He and his pilot landed and were able to walk just a few hundred yards to the water's edge. The lake was Lake Havasu, a 35 mile long reservoir developed by the Metropolitan Water District of Southern California. It is fed by the Colorado River and was created in 1938 by the completion of the Parker Dam.

The purpose of the lake was to provide water to Southern California (as it still does) but in the 60's and 70's, it was fast becoming a water playground for fishing and boating enthusiasts from Arizona and Southern California. The Colorado River is the border line between Arizona and California in this region and is within easy access from Southern California.

After making some serious inquiries about the lake and the land on the Arizona side of the lake, Mr. McCulloch purchased 3,353 acres and began to formulate a plan to build a city and move his manufacturing plants and employees from the area adjacent to Los Angeles International Airport to a desert town he named "Lake Havasu City".

McCulloch later negotiated with the Federal government and eventually was able to purchase an additional 13,000 acres of adjoining land. He formed a real estate sales division and as plans were being drawn and streets were being graded he began to advertise lots for sale.

Unlike many land sales deals in the 1960's, Mr. McCulloch wouldn't allow a lot to be sold unless the buyers came to Lake Havasu City, walked on the lot, and heard about his plans for a new city.

Because the 20-mile road to Lake Havasu City from Route 66 was not very good, he purchased a small fleet of passenger aircraft and flew qualified buyers in to see what was happening in this small desert city. He improved a World War II landing strip within a half-mile of "downtown" that served as Lake Havasu City Airport.

Although the desert area looked quite desolate to buyers coming from the eastern or mid-western states, they were greeted with the sunshine and warm winter weather after having just left their home in snow.

Guests on these free flights were given meals and overnight accommodations at the Havasu Hotel, built and operated by McCulloch Properties. The next morning was spent with a salesman looking at available lots. Many bought lots for their future retirement before flying home, but some bought lots, rented a place to stay and went home to pack.

If, after looking over Lake Havasu City they didn't buy a lot, they still got the flight home. But, if they did buy a lot, they got to fly back multiple times as long as they brought a friend or relative as a potential buyer with them.

The "Holly Flights", as they were called after the Holly Development Company, a sales enterprise formed by Robert McCulloch, started with several Lockheed Constellations, and then later purchased a fleet of eleven Electra Jets to bring people to view the fledgling Lake Havasu City. Mr. McCulloch demanded that the lots were sold strictly on a "see before you buy" basis.

Probably best known now, as "the American home for the London Bridge", Lake Havasu City made headlines when Robert McCulloch purchased the 1831-built London Bridge from the City of London in 1968. It was disassembled and shipped stone-by-stone through the Panama Canal to Long Beach, California, then trucked 300 miles to its new home.

The London Bridge was rebuilt on a peninsula, and upon completion, a channel was dredged under it allowing water to flow beneath the bridge from the Colorado River into Thompson Bay. The bridge was dedicated on October 10, 1971 with the Lord Mayor of London, the Governor of Arizona, and an estimated 50,000 spectators in attendance.

For many years after its completion, it was the second largest tourist attraction in Arizona; second only to the Grand Canyon in number of visitors. Today, it still is a major attraction with a constant flow of tourists coming to see it. Of course, the early attention was instrumental in selling lots over the years and today, 50 years after its founding, the town has a census population estimated at 52,000.

11

When we began our business in Lake Havasu City in 1993, we had just moved to the town from Tucson and were totally unknown. We had no relatives and no friends here prior to making the move. We had vacationed in the area since about 1969, but we spent most of our time on the Colorado River, near Parker, and about 35 miles from Lake Havasu City.

After leaving Tucson, we first tried living in Parker, with a population of about 3,000, but after a little more than a year, and our decision to start a tour business, it was obvious we needed to be in a larger city.

Lake Havasu City had the advantages of a larger, more affluent population, just 35 miles up the river and on the shores of Lake Havasu. That decision led to a very good and profitable nineteen years of business in this remote, Arizona city, known for its mild winter weather and for the London Bridge.

The London Bridge at Lake Havasu City during our January Balloon Fest.

Who Can Benefit From Reading This Book?

Anyone can benefit from reading this book that has a keen interest in travel and is willing to work hard to learn the business and earn the respect of potential travelers in his or her community. Operating a tour business can be very demanding, but also very rewarding when it is done right.

This is a perfect business for the young retired, especially successful sales professionals or others who like to talk and deal with people. Add to that a passion for travel and you have the perfect second career. As in my case, corporate retirement at age 53 and the tour business for another 19 years.

The reader should understand that it is impossible to start a tour business without some financial nest-egg to handle initial incorporation or LLC requirements, initial advertising, cost of scouting trips, liability insurance and some out-going deposits before you receive payments from your first customers.

A person who has recently retired from a corporate position with a good retirement and a reasonable financial nest egg is in a perfect position to start a tour business due to the fact that he or she will not need or expect an immediate return from the initial investment in start-up costs. This person may also have enough retirement income that the tour business income can be used to add to net worth.

Also, the owners of a young or struggling tour business can benefit from the many ideas in this book. Of course, not all my ideas will fit perfectly into someone else's situation. The differences in geographical location in relation to tour attractions, the availability of start-up funds, and the relative wealth of the area you have to draw from will influence the direction your tour business will take.

It is common for older retired people to choose to stay home because they don't want to or are unable to drive themselves. Often they don't have anyone offering to take them to interesting and exciting places for a reasonable fee. This is where you will come in by offering these senior adults a chance to travel with others in a safe, fun and exciting venue.

Lots of folks will jump at the chance to travel with a friendly group of people from their own town as long as they feel they will be well taken care of. Retired people are the primary market for group tours because they have the two necessary qualifications - time and money!

As you can see, the emphasis in this book is on **"senior adult leisure travel"**.

Other types of tour operations that some specialize in are "adventure travel", "student travel" and "religious travel".

"Adventure travel" is offering tours that involve an active sport such as snow skiing or scuba diving. Because of the inherent risk in this type of adventure, liability insurance is much different and considerably more expensive.

"Student travel" involves offering travel to student groups interested in studying the workings of government or visiting a key city, such as New York City or Washington, D.C. Chaperones are a necessary ingredient of any student travel.

"Religious travel" could include trips to the Holy Land and other places of religious significance. This is difficult to specialize in unless you have the opportunity to go state-wide or country-wide. Churches with large congregations can be a source for an occasional religious tour.

Although many of the aspects covered in this book might apply to these other areas of travel, the author has not had experience in these other areas and does not intend for the information in this book to necessarily apply to adventure, student or religious travel.

The Basics of the Tour Business

Definitions

What is a Tour Operator?

A person or company that provides package vacations.

Tour operators are individuals or businesses, small or large that combine two or more travel services such as transportation, accommodations, meals, entertainment, historical attractions and sightseeing and sell them as a package. Small tour operators generally sell their tours directly to travelers in their immediate area. The intent is to sell to individuals and couples that will form a group large enough to make the tour profitable.

The key to the definition above is that being a tour operator involves managing a business. A small, local tour operation like we had usually does not sell their packaged travel through travel agencies because to do that would mean that you would have to pay the travel agency a commission on each sale.

I found that in a smaller community, it is best to make yourself and your tour schedule known to the travel agencies and refer business to them when you have someone contact you about a trip that you are not offering. Once they see that you are not competing with them for individual travel, but in fact, you are sending business to them, they are more likely to tell people about your group tours.

Large, world-wide tour operators rely on the sales from travel agents and build in a percentage that they are glad to pay to the agencies that sell their tours. In a like manner, when you book a group on a tour with a large tour operator, they will either pay you a similar or better commission or will give you a net price (less 10-15% from the advertised price) for their product.

What is a Group Tour Operator?

Tour Operator and Group Tour Operator generally mean the same thing. A group tour operator is an individual or business, small or large that specializes in planning, organizing, marketing and conducting tours that are escorted and intended for groups of like-minded people. A group tour operator generally will not make arrangements for individuals' personal travel.

See Figure 1 in the Illustrations Section for a copy of the Bartlett Tours website and you will get an idea of what a Group Tour Operator offers.

Unfortunately, when we sold our business, I didn't think about capturing the latest version of our website. Naturally, the new owners of our business wanted to change it to reflect the change in ownership.

By the time I thought about writing this book and including screenshots of our web pages, the changes had been made. My webmaster had a copy of the website as of 2007 and that is the best we could find. So, even though the pages of our 2012 website would have the same look, the details in the written portion are dated.

An example of a group tour would be one to Washington, D.C., beginning from or meeting at a specific location on a specific date, visiting specified historical sites, conducted by a knowledgeable escort for a set price.

When this tour is advertised, it will draw travelers who are "like-minded" in that they have a desire to visit Washington, D.C. The tour operator will advertise the tour in various ways with the goal being to fill whatever type of vehicle he intends to use to move the group between the various historical sites.

In most cases, the vehicle will be a chartered bus, usually with 56 seats, but it could be a mini-bus, a 15-passenger van or a limousine.

Pricing of the group tour will depend on the number of travelers that the group tour operator has designed the tour to accommodate. Naturally, if the fixed costs of the tour (the cost of bus charter usually being the single biggest fixed cost) can be spread over a larger number of travelers the cost per traveler will be lower and more attractive.

Charter bus companies charge for the time and distance a bus must travel, whether there are 10 passengers or 50 passengers.

What is a Tour Director or Tour Manager?

A Tour Director, sometimes known as a Tour Manager, is the person in total charge of a tour. They may be the owner of the company or they may be an employee of the tour company and must be capable of leading the tour for several days or weeks. The Tour Director may do the entire narration of the tour, but more likely will have various "step-on guides" provide day or half-day tours of their specific areas or cities.

The Tour Director is responsible for keeping the tour on time, for seeing that the travelers are happy and well informed, and that the tour covers all of the elements that were advertised in the travel brochure. Handling any accidents or injuries that happen on tour is also the responsibility of the Tour Director.

On our tours, I was the Tour Director and I had full responsibility for the success of each tour. For the most part, this was an enjoyable task, but when there was a lost bag or a sick passenger, it became necessary to get very serious about solving the immediate problem without alarming the other travelers.

What is a Step-On Guide?

A step-on guide is a person available for hire that is an expert on their city, state or national park, or area. A step-on guide generally has a set rate by the hour, half-day or full-day to provide detailed information about a specific area of interest. They will be positioned at the front of the bus pointing out things of interest and giving facts and figures while directing each turn for the driver.

Step-on guides add a great deal to a tour. They add their own personal facts about the area that a person not from the area would be hard pressed to know. They survive on their pay from the tour company, but they are also highly dependent on tips from the group. I always encouraged our travelers to tip about $2.00 per person for a half-day tour and about $4.00 for a full day tour.

What is a Driver-Narrator?

A Driver-Narrator is often found on Gray Line and other city sightseeing tours. As the title infers, the person narrating the tour is also the driver of the vehicle. They work for the tour company and are paid but also depend on tips from their passengers.

For instance, if you are flying your group to a destination like Washington, D.C. or San Antonio, Texas, you might use a company like Gray Line to handle your charter transportation and your tours while you are there.

Generally, you can depend on local tour companies being able to show a high level of knowledge of the city and often they are able to get access to tours of important buildings or sites that would be difficult, if not impossible, for you to do as an independent tour company.

What is a Receptive Operator?

A receptive operator is a locally based tour operator in a destination that regularly experiences large numbers of tour or convention groups. For instance, convention cities like Miami Beach, San Francisco and Las Vegas would fit in this category.

A receptive operator, sometimes called a destination management company, can be utilized by a travel agency, a corporation or an organization to handle all aspects of a group coming to visit that city, including greeters, registration personnel, lodging, meals, transportation, sightseeing tours, activities, meeting or banquet space and recreation.

A receptive operator would not generally be used by a tour operator as defined in this book but would more likely by used by a corporation having a convention; a school or college group on a field trip; or a club or organization with a specific interest in the locale.

What is a Pre-Formed Group?

A group tour operator may, on occasion, conduct a tour that is requested by a "pre-formed" group. A pre-formed group could be members of a church, an Elks club, a genealogy club, or any number of other community groups that have a desire to travel to a site or location that is of interest to them. They may contact one or several tour operators for a price on a tour for their group. In some cases, if their trip is quite simple, they may go directly to a charter bus company for transportation and take care of all the other details of their travel themselves.

A warning about dealing with pre-formed groups: In most cases there is a "ringleader" who has come up with the idea of this trip and has "sold" it to the others in his or her group. This person has taken ownership of the trip and could be difficult to work with when trade-offs or compromise is necessary.

 If you are asked, as a tour operator, to design the tour, select the lodging and arrange the meals, it is imperative that you get the leader to sign off and approve your choices ahead of time and in writing and only after receiving a deposit sufficient to cover your effort in case of cancellation.

The worst thing you can face, as an escort on tour, is the leader who wants to make changes during the tour. If you put yourself in the position of accepting changes along your route, you will be flying "by the seat of your pants" and reservations you have made in advance may be jeopardized. Changing the tour route changes your timing for rest stops, attractions and your final destination for the day.

If the club or organization is intending to offer the trip for a per-person fee, there must be a significant deposit or better yet, a requirement that each person must pay in full upon making their reservation. If they later must cancel, it should be their responsibility or the responsibility of the organization to re-sell their space.

In my business, I chose not to deal with pre-formed groups due to the risk to my business reputation and due to the fact that this pre-formed group tour would be a distraction from my scheduled tours. Instead, I would direct them to a charter bus company and let the bus company handle it.

Ingredients for the Success of a Tour Operator

Statistics show that 55% of new businesses fail within the first 5 years of operation. This research was published in *Entrepreneur Weekly*, July 27, 2013 and was conducted by the Small Business Development Center at the University of Tennessee.

The good news is that with the proper ingredients, you can be one of the 45% that succeed. Although every business has its differences, there are 12 ingredients that every tour business and its owners should recognize.

1) A Strong Personality and Good Speaking Ability

If you find it easy to talk with people, can explain things clearly and are somewhat of a "salesman", the tour business could be a natural for you. When you're on the road with a tour group, you are the leader and you must be clear and forceful with any instructions you give.

The people on your tour will look to you to guide them in every facet of the tour. This includes setting the time for each days' departure, rest stops (with a time to be back on the bus ready to roll), what you recommend they do during free time, and a myriad of other instructions each day of the tour.

With a smile on my face, I've always told my tour groups, "this is not a democracy – it is a benevolent dictatorship, and I'm the dictator".

I'm sorry, but if you aren't comfortable around people and have a difficult time talking with people, the tour business is not for you. Being a strong leader can be especially important when there is a crisis on a tour. The leader must take charge in the event of an injury, a bus breakdown, a lost member of the tour, etc. and must make the others feel that the situation is under control.

2) Good Destination Possibilities

A tour business must have a good "product". This is the most important element of any business. The product, in the case of a tour operation, is the destination. The tour destination can be as simple as a museum or a theme park for a one-day trip. If the tour is longer than one day, you may have several destinations with at least one major destination that will be the "draw" in your advertising.

In most cases, the destination must be an attraction that most people in your area have heard about, such as Mount Rushmore, or the Rose Parade, and be reasonably accessible by bus or airplane, or both, from your starting point.

Ideally, there should be numerous tour attractions within a traveling distance of one day or less, approximately 300-350 miles, in various directions from your base location. This gives you the opportunity to have one or several attractions in the course of a two or three day tour.

3) A Business Plan

Every successful business, no matter how large or small, starts with a plan. A Business Plan will help you plan your strategies and map your direction. Without a clear and concise plan of action, it's easy to lose sight of where your business is headed and where you want it to go.

At a minimum, a business plan for a tour operation should start with a very short sentence or two describing your concept of the business, then continue with who your prospective customers will be, your possible destinations, how you will transport your travelers, the management of the business and form of ownership, an analysis of the market as you see it, your plan for marketing your tours and your financial plan for at least the first year.

A business plan of just a few pages will get you started. I still have mine from 1992 and it was three pages. I laugh now because I restricted the business to tours of Southern Arizona and the Southwest. Little did I know at that time, that within a few years we would be taking our travelers to Alaska, Canada, Mexico, Hawaii, Britain, Europe, Australia, Tahiti, China, and beyond.

One of the programs on the market offering a template for writing business plans is Growthink www.growthink.com. They offer a free version and an expanded version for less than $100. Although I have not used this template, their website is very interesting and they offer a 365 day satisfaction guarantee. By using their template, they advertise that you can put together a business plan in just a few hours. Google "business plans" and you will get many more options.

4) Desire and Determination

Owning a tour business is serious business. Owning your own business is a far cry from working for someone or even running someone else's business. As a business owner, everything that affects the business, affects you. If you're like most of us, you're putting all that you have into your business.

Owning a business can be quite stressful, and sometimes you might even question whether it's all worth it. But that's where your determination and desire kick in. Being knowledgeable about and enjoying what you do also is a benefit. If you enjoy what you do, the difficult days aren't so bad and can often serve as a learning experience.

5) Customer Base

Of course, if you don't have customers, you don't have sales. Your customer base should be the people your tour business will appeal to. In most cases, unless you are specializing in high adventure or ski trips, your customer base is going to be retired people who have some disposable income or savings to spend on travel.

Knowing who your customers are is very important. Your local Chamber of Commerce can be of help in defining the number of retired people in your community and other surrounding communities and their approximate income range.

Often those who are retired but have tired of traveling in their own motorhome or fifth-wheel are great prospects for bus tours, cruises and tours outside of the United States. These people have a strong interest in travel but are now at the point in their lives where they want someone else to plan their trips and drive for them.

6) Internet/Web Site

In today's world, it seems that everyone says you have to have a website. If your tour business is going to be limited to your town or city and the surrounding area, you can get away without a website while you are building your business. However, a professional, easy to navigate website shows that you are a professional business and that you want your travelers to be able to view your schedule at their convenience.

If you have someone who is local and has a reputation for developing good-looking websites, that may be your best bet. If not, check out online website developers such as The Web Weaver www.thewebweaver.com . If you're looking for somewhere to register your domain name and have your site hosted, try www.doteasy.com or www.godaddy.com .

Check with your service provider to determine if you can host your website on the personal space you already have with them, rather than paying a company a fee for hosting your website. My website was developed for me by a high school friend, was hosted on my ISP without a fee and was regularly used by many of my customers.

My tour business has had a website since 2001 and the new owners have continued with a similar website. However, since my business was very local, I estimate I only received about 5-10% of my reservations via the website. Even if a potential customer looked at the website for information, when they wanted to place a reservation they most often called and talked to me.

I liked talking with potential clients, because the tour business in a small community is a very personal business. Talking with a new prospect on the phone gave me a chance to learn about them and possibly make them more comfortable by giving them a feel for how we took care of our travelers.

7) *Advertising and Marketing*

For your tour business to survive, people have to know that you exist. Every successful business must do some form of advertising or marketing. You should have established a first year advertising budget in your business plan.

If you live in a town or city that has a daily newspaper, placing an ad there is probably where you should start. Resist advertising on restaurant place mats even though you will be the only tour business on that mat. I have not found that type of advertising to be effective. If you have a local radio station that is listened to by senior adults, advertising there could work well for you. Even a local swap meet could be a good place to meet people and hand out your tour schedule.

8) Excellent Customer Service

No matter how many customers you get, if you don't take care of them they will leave, and most likely they won't be back. Even worse, they might tell others not to do business with you. In the tour business, I sincerely believe that the most potent form of advertising is "word of mouth". You may have competition in your town or nearby. Your level of customer service can make the difference in someone traveling with you or traveling with someone else.

Make each customer feel as though they are your most important customer. You'll find that they will return and, in most cases, they will also send others to you. Be sure to answer every email and every call promptly.

9) Employees

Every tour business has to have employees, even if it's only one. No business can run itself. You must run and handle your business professionally. Some small business owners, especially home based businesses, seem to forget that it's still a business. In most cases, you won't need to keep regular office hours for a tour business. If prospective travelers want to see you in person, make a scheduled appointment and meet them in your home or theirs.

If you are inviting people into your home, it's best to have a room set aside as your office and make it look as business-like as possible. Meeting customers at your kitchen table does not make your business look professional or permanent, especially if someone is busy cooking dinner. Most people will mail their payment to you rather than dropping it off, so having people visit you will be an occasional rather than a regular event.

10) Customer Records

A successful tour business, more than most other businesses, thrives on repeat customers. Therefore, it is crucial to keep a record of each person that has requested your schedule or signed up for a tour. In today's world, it is imperative that these records be kept on a computer system so that you can automate such menial tasks as printing mailing labels, badges, luggage tags, boarding passes and guest lists.

Each customer record should show the date it was started, name(s), address, city, state, zip, phone number (both local and cell), the list of tours taken, special needs or requests, etc. I'll be more specific and show my actual record layout later in this book.

11) Accounting/Finance

Every business must have a system for handling finances. There must be a process for receiving and disbursing money. You must also consider how you'll pay hotels, restaurants, vendors, charter bus companies, etc. In today's world, a business credit card seems to be the best answer.

Most hotels and many restaurants and attractions prefer a credit card to a check because they don't have to worry about the validity of the payment. I used a Capital One credit card that after a few years earned a credit limit of $40,000. I liked Capital One because of the Rewards Points I earned that could be used for our scouting travel.

Because the tour business is one that traditionally collects all payments from the travelers at least 30 days in advance of the tour, there is no Accounts Receivable (a customer owing you after the product is delivered). I operated my business from 1993 until 2012 by taking only personal checks and occasional cash. People would occasionally ask about using a credit card but I always said, "I'm just keeping my business simple – your personal check is fine".

I began to see, however, with our "cashless society", that I was going to have to change or possibly lose business. Fortunately, I sold the business before that needed to happen. The new owner of Bartlett Tours has decided, after a year of business that he will take credit cards but asks for a fee of 1.5% (his cost for processing) for using the card.

A tour business has no Accounts Payable since most hotels and restaurants will either charge your credit card a month in advance or upon your group arrival. If the business will be run by the owners, there will probably be no payroll.

One of the best and most user friendly small business accounting packages is Quicken, available at www.shopintuit.com, Amazon.com or Staples.

 I found Quicken easy to learn and it has the capability of keeping track of expenses by type and by the individual tour. I still have all income and expenses available on Quicken back to the time I began using it in January 1994.

12) Insurance and Legal Protection

Don't consider running your first tour without liability insurance! I saved this one for last because it is one of the most important ingredients, but probably the least thought about. Although my tour business never had a lawsuit or an insurance claim in 19 years, I still paid for liability insurance every year.

I recommend insurance specific to the tour operators needs. This insurance will cover claims from a guest who may fall or injure themselves on one of your tours as well as from negligent acts on your part or "errors and omissions" in your advertisements or customer communications.

The cost of the insurance is generally determined by your projected gross income over the next year and whether or not you intend to offer any "adventure" type travel. Adventure travel would include skiing, white-water rafting, hang gliding, scuba diving and other high level and injury-prone activities. This type of activity should be left to an adventure specialized tour company.

There are several companies that offer specific tour operator coverage. I started with The Berkely Agency, **www.Berkely.com** in 1993 and stayed with them. They offer a "Travel Agents and Tour Operators Professional Liability Insurance Policy" that covers the following:

> Bodily Injury and Property Damage
> Professional Liability (includes negligent acts & negligent omissions)
> Personal Injury
> Fire & Legal Liability

The rate for this liability insurance is based on your estimate of gross income over the next year, so the cost will start out quite low.

If you rent a parking lot, you can protect the owners of the lot from one of your travelers hurting themselves while in the parking lot by adding the owner as an "additional insured" on your liability policy, generally for no additional premium.

While we're on the subject of insurance, it's a good idea to ask your charter bus provider to include your company as an "additional insured" as well, so that if someone sues you and the bus charter company for an injury occurrence on board the bus, you will be covered by the bus company's insurance.

Ask the bus company to send you a "Certificate of Liability Insurance" from their insurer showing you as that "additional insured". Occasionally, a hotel or attraction that you will be using will ask to see your bus company's insurance, and you can send this certificate to them as proof. Once you request this proof, the insurance company will automatically send you an update each year.

You should consider separating your business and its assets from your personal assets. If you intend to make the tour business the source of your primary or secondary income, you should consider organizing your business as a Limited Liability Company (LLC) or an "S" Corporation.

The reason for organizing your tour business this way is to limit your liability and not put your personal assets at risk in case of a lawsuit. Make sure to have a talk with your accountant or a lawyer for advice on this matter.

Owning a business is not the easiest thing to do, but it is not the most difficult either. No one can guarantee your success in business, except you. Your success is totally dependent upon you and how you handle your business, but utilizing these 12 ingredients improves your chances. Your business will not likely survive without them.

Analyzing Your Market

If you are reading this book, you probably have a desire to start a tour business in the town in which you live now. In that case, you probably know a lot about your town or city and believe you can analyze the market based on your own knowledge as a local citizen. However, even if you have lived there all your life, you probably wouldn't know what percentage of your town's population are over 55 (the prime target for a local tour operator) or what percentage are retired.

One place to start to gather information about your market is your local Chamber of Commerce. They will likely have information about population by age category, by job type, by average earnings per household, etc. based on the last census. Ask them if they know of any tour company in the vicinity, since you want to know if you will have competition right from the start.

If your town has a Senior Center, go there and talk with the manager of the center and see if he or she thinks that seniors that frequent the center would be interested in taking tours if they didn't have to drive to the "big city" to start the tour, but instead left from a convenient parking lot right in your area.

With the wide range of information you can get today off the Internet, I would encourage you to search for more data about the area you live in. Try entering the following on Google or your favorite search engine: "what are the population statistics for Clinton, Iowa".

This will get you started, but other excellent tools are "www.areavibes.com" and "clrsearch.com" (click on demographics rather than real estate). Both of these will show you graphs of the population by age categories if you scroll down far enough. If your town is small but there are other small towns within 60 miles (a one hour drive), you will want to include them in your potential customer count.

An Example: I used the above tools to analyze the potential for a tour business in a small city that my wife and I visited on a personal trip recently – Clinton, Iowa. Using a combination of the three sources listed above, I determined the following:

The population of Clinton, Iowa as of 2010 to be 26,885
13.62% of the population is over 65 years of age (our target audience)
US population over 55 years of age is 10.2%
There are no commercial flights out of Clinton, Iowa

What these figures can tell you is that you have a potential market segment of about 3,600 people over 65 years of age. Our experience is that the age group most likely to travel on a bus tour or cruise is over the age of 65 (we had several who still traveled with us into their 90's).

Since you can normally only count on 5 to 10% of these "eligible" people to travel with you, doing business just in this one town probably would not be feasible if you wanted to conduct 5-10 tours each year. So, in this instance, you would need to go further and analyze the markets of the other small towns up to 60 miles away. My research found that there are 15 towns within 25 miles of Clinton, certainly close enough to be attracted to your tours.

You may think that not having any commercial flights out of your city is a problem if you might eventually want to take your groups to another part of the United States or on a cruise or to a destination overseas. Actually, I found that having no commercial airline flights from my town was a significant advantage to my business.

Many older individuals dislike airports (especially since the strict security requirements after 9/11) and as they have gotten older they have given up trying to go anywhere that requires driving a distance to the airport, finding a parking place with all the confusing signs, and going through security.

Lake Havasu City, where we live and where our tour business was located, is 150 miles from the closest commercial airport, Las Vegas; 200 miles from Phoenix Sky Harbor Airport; and 330 miles from Los Angeles International Airport. This requires us to leave our town by chartered bus (often with an overnight hotel stay because of a morning departure) and go through the airport as a group.

I make sure I tell my groups what to expect, first in writing with their final invoice and then verbally on the way to the airport. Going through an airport is like playing a game. If you don't understand the rules of the game, it makes little sense and can be very intimidating. But, if someone explains the rules, it becomes familiar, interesting and even exciting. The same is true with an airport for our travelers.

The comment I get after we are through security and are waiting at the gate is often, "well, that was easy". Of course, we allow plenty of time to check in as a group so that there is never a fear of missing the plane. This means we arrive at check-in two hours ahead for a domestic flight and three hours for an international flight.

The hidden advantage of <u>not</u> having a local commercial airport is that a single person or a couple will be more likely to go with you - someone they know and trust who will help them understand "the rules". In addition, being with a group of similar aged individuals, with a strong leader, takes a lot of the fear out of travel.

For the tour operator, the advantage is that there is a profit opportunity in the effort of getting the group to the plane that wouldn't be there if everybody just met at the airport. I will explain more about this factor later.

The 15 Steps to Your First Tour

1. IDENTIFY THE DESTINATION

Choose a simple destination, possible to travel to and visit in one or two days.

2. PREPARE A TOUR ITINERARY

Use a paper map or a computer mapping program.

3. SCOUT THE TOUR

Get in your car and stop at all the places in your itinerary. Get prices and make adjustments where necessary.

4. PICK A FIRM TOUR DATE

Allow at least two to three months to sell the tour.

5. ARRANGE FOR A CHARTER BUS

Check out a 15-passenger van rental, just in case. If your final count is as low as 8 or 9, you should still be able to show a profit with a rented van.

6. CALCULATE YOUR TOUR PRICE

Gather all your costs and add a profit factor.

7. MAKE FIRM RESERVATIONS

Contract for bus charter, hotels (if any), and dining, plus any attractions and entertainment.

8. ADVERTISE

Get the word out about your exciting new tour!

9. PRODUCE A MAILER & E-MAILER

Produce a sales piece with a detailed description of the tour that you will send to those that call or email as a result of your advertising.

10. GATHER INFO FROM RESPONSES

Begin your mailing list from these first calls. If the caller doesn't go on this tour, they may go with you later.

11. COLLECT DEPOSITS

Keep track of the deposits received from your mailings. This will be the indicator of whether this tour is a "go".

12. PURCHASE LIABILITY INSURANCE

Don't leave home without it! But, don't buy it before you know your first tour is a definite "go".

13. Send confirmation letters and request final balances.

Now, watch the money start rolling in!

14. Confirm, confirm, confirm!

Make doubly sure that all your reservations are firm!

15. Conduct the tour and have a ball!

You're on your way!
On this tour, start selling your next tour.

Now, read the next few chapters for the details in applying
"The 15 Steps to your First Tour".

Identifying Tour Possibilities

If you have been giving any thought at all to starting a tour business, you probably have a few destinations in mind already. These may be places you and your family have been to, places co-workers have mentioned and ads or articles you've seen in magazines, travel brochures or in searches for tours on the Internet.

My advice is to start making a list of these possible destinations. I would suggest that for your first few tours you pick a destination that can be done in one day or two days with an overnight. This will allow you to get some experience and the low price will be an encouragement to local travelers who may not know you but will be willing to take a chance on a relatively low-cost tour offered by you.

Possibilities for Short Tours:

- Historical Museums
- Musical Productions and Stage Shows
- Casinos and Entertainers appearing at Casinos
- Theme Parks
- Patriotic Celebrations
- Wineries and Wine Tastings
- Agricultural and Farm Tours
- Rodeos and Horse Shows
- Scenic Areas and Fall Color
- Town Celebrations and Parades
- Scenic and Historic Train Rides
- Balloon Festivals
- State and County Fairs
- Day River Excursions
- Factory Tours
- National and State Parks
- Historic Mansions and Plantations
- Famous Gardens
- City Tours of cities in your tour area

Naturally, if you are in a very remote location, like we are, you may not be able to get to an attraction, spend some time there, and then return in one day. People may not want to ride for six or eight hours on a bus just to spend a few hours at a museum or event. If this is the case, you need to plan other stops, interesting stops, at reasonable intervals along the way and design the tour as an overnight trip.

If your clients are older (as they most likely will be), they would much rather spend a little more to stay overnight than to arrive back in their town late at night. Also, if your closest bus charter company is in a large city some miles away, the "deadhead" charge (the charge for bus and driver to come to you empty and return empty) may make a one-day tour cost prohibitive.

Speaking of charter buses (sometimes called "motorcoaches" with the luxury they offer today), be sure you determine where you will charter your bus from and the exact cost before you advertise your first tour. The bus charter will often be the largest single cost in your tour.

The word "charter" means to "hire a means of transportation" to include a professional driver with a Commercial Drivers License (CDL). This is different from "renting" a vehicle where you, the renter, take on the responsibility of driving. Buses are not available for rent. I will talk more about buses later.

Preparing a Preliminary Tour Itinerary

Once you have decided on a first tour, it's time to work on a tour itinerary. When I first started our company in 1993, I used regular paper maps and added up mileage as I went along. This may still be the way you begin your tour business.

Let's assume you are planning a two-day tour with an overnight about six hours away. Using a paper map of your state or area, begin at the place you will be meeting your group and where you will be departing from. Follow the map in the direction of your destination until you have determined the "best" route to your destination.

This may mean that you will route it along the fastest highway or you may determine that you will take a slower, scenic route if the distance to your destination allows it. Once you have determined the route, go back over the route looking for stops for restroom breaks (about every two hours) and a place for lunch. Of course, you may not be able to find these places from your map. This is why a scouting trip is necessary before you conduct the tour.

If at all possible, I like to make the return trip via a different route than the first day. This not only makes the travel more interesting for your guests, but gives you the opportunity for interesting commentary about the history, or the people along the way.

Using a Computer Mapping Program

I prefer to do this planning using Microsoft *Streets & Trips*, an inexpensive computer mapping program available for less than $60.

Start by picking the major stops along the way. This will include stops for meals, attractions and overnight stays. Start the *Streets & Trips* program by selecting "Route Planner" (click on the image of a brown car heading toward you – 2010 version).

First, enter your address or your town as the starting point. Now, start typing the address, the town or the name of the attraction into the "type place or address" box at the left side of *Streets & Trips*.

See Figure 2 in the Illustrations Section for a screenshot of *Streets & Trips*.

After typing each one into the box, click on "Add to route". At any time, you can click on "Get Directions" and the program will show you a blue-line map and turn-by-turn directions along with total miles and total driving time.

As well as showing the mileage at each point, it will show you the time of arrival based on the type of highway or road you are traveling on. You can change the speeds for each road type, but using "average" seems to work well. The program adjusts with higher speeds on highways and freeways and lower speeds on country roads and still lower on city streets.

Streets & Trips allows you to change the start time for each day (default start time is 9:00am) and the latest time you want to be traveling (default time is 5:00pm). It also allows you to enter the total time you want to spend at any stop (i.e. 20 minutes for a restroom break, 1 hour 15 minutes for lunch, 1 night for an overnight, etc.) so that you can quickly see the time estimated for each arrival and departure.

Adding times for a stop is done easily by clicking on the stop name to highlight it, then clicking on the small clock in the same block just under "Reverse Route". After clicking on the clock, you will see that there are three options: Stop for…, Arrive at…, Depart at… However, if you have highlighted the last town or attraction on your list, you won't have the options available since the program sees this as your final destination. You will need to add other destinations before you can use the clock feature.

Once you have the "major" stops entered, go back and find the points that will work for a restroom break. Generally, you want to make a restroom stop every two hours, but no longer than 2 ½ hours. Sometimes the lack of a suitable rest stop will force you to take a different route.

You can enter these stops into the itinerary by typing the town name and clicking. This will add the location of the rest stop to the itinerary, but it may be in the wrong sequence. Click on the rest stop name to highlight it and then click on the up arrow to move it one position per click. An easier way is to find the town on the *Streets & Trips* map, right click on it, then select "Add as stop", and the town will be entered in the proper sequence.

Note that I am providing only very basic instructions on the use of Microsoft *Streets & Trips*. Once you have purchased the product, click on "Help", and then click on "Streets & Trips on the Web". This will take you to a Microsoft site that has help for the beginner. You may also go on the Internet and find one of several tutorials that are provided with or without video and learn all you can do with this powerful mapping program.

Go to Figure 3 to see a detailed listing of the route with stops provided by Microsoft *Streets & Trips*.

Continue to enter the various stops that you have in mind for your tour. Use the clock feature to enter your overnight stays. Click on "Stop for...", then click the down arrow on "Hrs:Mins" and click on "Nights", then enter 1 or more nights that you plan to stay at that location.

Keep in mind that at this point in your planning you probably won't know exactly where you will be eating or staying. Instead, you are just doing a rough layout of your tour plan to see if it fits together well. If you have a long day of travel, use the

Internet to see if you can find an attraction that could be added that would be interesting and would break up the time on the bus.

When you have entered all the major stops along the way, and entered times for each stop, click on "Get Directions" to study the flow of your tour. The first time you do this you may find that one day is too long and another day is too short. This will require you to move the overnight to make the days more equal.

You may also find that you have too much activity crammed into a two day tour, so you have to consider either taking something out or making it a three day tour. Any changes, like lengthening a tour, have consequences in pricing that have to be taken into consideration.

Bus tours vary widely in price per day depending on the cost of the bus charter, the quality of overnight accommodations, dining, and the number of people you expect to take. The bus charter cost will be the same whether you take twenty guests or fifty. Most other costs will be per-person.

Including Meals While on Tour

As a matter of policy, our tours always included dinners. We ate either in a group setting in a banquet room at the hotel or at a nice restaurant not far from the hotel. Occasionally, our dinners would be at a restaurant in route to our hotel if the distance dictated that. In most cases, we stayed at quality motels that offered a breakfast, usually with one or two hot items.

We always included dinner each evening so that we never put our guests, a majority of which were women, in the position of going out of the hotel on their own to find a place to eat. We arranged a banquet dinner in the hotel, used the bus to take everyone to a restaurant, or provided vouchers for our travelers to eat "at their leisure" at a restaurant in the hotel. In all cases, the dinner as well as the gratuity was paid by us, not the guest.

If we needed to stay in a more expensive hotel that had a restaurant (and therefore did not offer a free breakfast), we included that breakfast in the cost of the tour. Most people will shy away from a breakfast in a hotel that costs $15 or more, but don't have a problem with eating it if the high price is "buried" in the total cost of the tour. In fact, in most cases they view this as a nice feature of a high-quality tour.

We also provided lunches unless there was a stop where our guests could have a choice of several places to eat, such as in a historic downtown area. We stayed away from fast-food restaurants unless we absolutely had to, because we wanted to portray a higher image for our tours. Even in small towns, we were often able to find a café or restaurant that was happy to provide a soup and sandwich lunch to a group of 45-50 people.

Sample Prices of Tours

In our last fifteen months of business, January 2011-March 2012, our price for one popular overnight trip (2 days) was $319, or $159.50 per day. This was a trip to Palm Springs, California to see a very popular and patriotic variety show called the Palm Springs Follies. We also included a visit to the Palm Springs Air Museum or a city tour as well as one breakfast and one dinner.

We conducted four three-day tours in 2012. The prices for each were:

- Death Valley & Scotty's Castle at $549 ($183/day);

- A Broadway shows tour to Tuacahn Amphitheatre near St. George, Utah at $399 ($133/day);

- A tour to Sedona, Arizona and a scenic train ride, The Verde River Train, for $519 ($173/day);

- A Southern California Christmas Shows tour at $495 ($165/day).

The bus charter cost for these four tours ranged from $3,757 to $4,500 ($1,252 to $1,500 per day) due to differences in total miles driven.

Remember, that this charter cost included a 200-mile deadhead each way, from and to Phoenix before and after the actual tour. However, for the Tuacahn tour, we used a bus company out of Las Vegas, so the deadhead was about 150 miles each way. It also involved housing each driver overnight in the motel next to our parking lot before the trip started the next morning.

Scouting your Tours

When you have decided on your first tour, the next thing to do is plan a scouting trip. This means that you actually travel the route of the trip, stopping at points of interest to determine if each would make a good and interesting stop for your tour guests.

Restroom Stops

One of the most important things to keep in mind while scouting a tour is the location of restrooms. You might think restrooms? Don't modern buses all have restrooms on board? Yes, all modern tour buses (as opposed to city buses or mini-buses) do have restrooms.

But, picture this: You may have 50 people, mostly seniors, on board. Beginning about two hours after you have started out, more than one person is going to feel the "urge". If you have already briefed them on the schedule for the day, and they know a restroom stop is coming up soon, they will wait.

However, if you haven't made it clear when you will be stopping, someone will start the parade to the restroom in the back of the bus. When one person starts this, others begin to think about the same thing. Soon, you're going to have a log-jam at the back of the bus and people are going to be unhappy.

Although the restroom on the bus is always available, I announce at the beginning of each tour that we will be stopping approximately every 2 hours and that the restroom at the back of the bus should only be used in a "can't wait" emergency. Using my itinerary, I give them the expected time for our first restroom break.

I explain that this is for two important reasons – first, we have planned rest stops along the way; and second, there is a danger having people walking down the aisle while the bus is in motion. If the driver has to swerve or hit the brakes, a person in the aisle, especially an older person, is very likely to fall and could easily be hurt.

Plan your itinerary to make a restroom stop every two to two and a half hours along the way. If the route makes it necessary to go longer than two hours, I always let my travelers know before they get off the bus at the stop prior and encourage them to stop at the restrooms before they get back on the bus.

Make sure the place you stop at has multiple fixtures in each restroom, as most freeway rest areas, convenience stores, modern truck stops and attractions do. In some cases, we have stopped at a McDonald's for a morning restroom break. It also gives people a chance to have a cup of coffee or other snack before moving on.

Scouting one of our tours into California, we could not find a suitable restroom in or near Bakersfield along the way. After stopping at a couple of older truck stops that did not meet our standards, we got inventive and checked out a very modern Amtrak station that was near the freeway and it worked very well. In addition, the train station had some interesting features that everyone enjoyed seeing and it turned out to be more than just a rest stop.

Finding Interesting Stops along the Way

Before your scouting trip you need to spend some serious time researching the route on the Internet. At this point, you should know what the major destination or event is that you are designing this tour around. In a multi-day tour, there may be several key stops along the way.

Now is the time to begin a search for interesting stops or highlights along the way. While looking at a map of your proposed route, use Google to search each little town your route will cross. Often you'll find that towns have a historic building, a small museum or a landscape feature that could be an interesting stop or at least could be something to mention as you pass by on the highway.

When you know that you are close to a 2-hour point on your map (120 to 140 miles depending on the type of road), check the towns for a convenience store or a truck stop to be your restroom break. If you are traveling a highway or freeway that has rest areas, they are usually marked on the map by a small green circle with a pyramid inside.

These rest areas can be found on a regular paper map or you can Google, for example, "rest areas in New Mexico" and find them usually listed by highway number. Rest areas are usually the best place to stop along the way if they appear at the right time in your schedule.

If you are using *Streets & Trips*, try "find nearby places" indicated by a green map pin in the upper ribbon on your screen. You can select "rest areas" and the distance around a point or city, and it will show you any that are along the roadside. This aid can also be used to find hotels/motels, restaurants, parks, etc. by selecting these from an extensive list.

Sometimes, you need to adjust the start time of your day in accordance with your morning restroom stop and your lunch stop. For example, if your lunch stop is 200 miles from your morning departure point and the freeway allows travel at 70 miles per hour, you can estimate about three hours of driving time and 20 minutes for a rest stop.

If you were planning to leave at 8:00am, this would put you into your lunch stop about 11:20am. This would be good timing for the first day of your tour because people will have eaten early to get to your group meeting place well before departure. However, an 11:20am lunch might be too early if this is a day in the middle of your tour and you planned to provide a full breakfast before leaving.

Delaying the departure from 8:00am to 9:00am would provide a more leisurely morning and would put you into your lunch stop at about 12:20. The time of departure should be flexible and must be adjusted to fit the other events of the day.

As I mentioned earlier, since about the year 2000 I have used Microsoft *Streets and Trips*, a mapping program on my computer to route each tour. I use and find it very helpful in the early planning for a new tour. It provides accurate mileage and timing for each point along the way.

See Figure 2 for a screenshot of *Streets and Trips.*

Microsoft *Streets and Trips* allows you the flexibility to have multiple days, different start times each day, and a specific length of time at each stop or event. I start by entering the start and stop locations for each day, then I add potential lunch stops, rest stops and attraction stops as I determine them from my own knowledge or from Internet research.

Try to make this itinerary as complete as you can before you leave for your scouting trip then make changes or corrections along the way. If you have this program on a laptop, you can make the changes to the mapping program while you are scouting. If not, you should take good notes along the way and update the map on the mapping program when you return home.

I did the routing of our tours for the first 6 or 7 years, starting in 1993, with just an Auto Club map of the state, a calculator and a pencil, but if you try a mapping program, you'll find it much easier and more accurate.

A few weeks before the actual tour, I use the print-out from the mapping program to produce a less detailed itinerary for my use and for the driver. I send this to the bus company at least a week before the tour so that the driver has a chance to look it over before the tour.

See Figure 4 for the less detailed itinerary for the driver and myself.

I put my copy of the itinerary on a clip board that I use on the bus to track our timing and make sure I keep the tour on time. I also make notes of the <u>actual</u> timing (rather than my computer timing) so that I can adjust these times for the next time we might do this same tour.

To produce a tour route map and the detailed itinerary with timings for our 3-day Death Valley tour required that I enter the 17 stops along the way into the Route Planner. The 17 stops were entered exactly as follows (notes in italics are added for explanation):

1. Lake Havasu City (dep 7:15am AZ time)	*Start of tour*
2. Searchlight, NV (20 minutes)	*Truck Stop Restroom*
3. Fiesta Henderson Casino (depart 11:15am NV)	*Buffet Lunch*
4. Amargosa Valley, NV	*(for routing)*
5. Death Valley Junction	*Tour of Opera House*
6. Furnace Creek Ranch	*Dinner, overnight, brkfst*
7. Badwater	*½ day Lower Valley Tour*
8. Furnace Creek Inn	*Historic tour & Lunch*
9. Furnace Creek Ranch	*Museum & Free time*
10. Stovepipe Wells Village	*Depart 6:00pm - Dinner*
11. Furnace Creek Ranch	*Overnight, breakfast*
12. Scotty's Castle	*Scheduled tour*
13. Junction 287 & 95	*(for routing)*
14. Rhyolite NV	*Ghost Town Drive Thru*
15. Beatty NV Casino	*Rest Stop*
16. Fiesta Henderson Casino	*Buffet Dinner*
17. Lake Havasu City	*End of tour*

I always put into my tour itinerary a little "fudge" factor each day. For instance, if I see we are running a little bit late due to traffic or road work or just "because", I can adjust the time for lunch down from an hour and a half to an hour and fifteen minutes.

The one problem I have with computer mapping programs is that they produce a very, very detailed trip plan. The program may print a line to advise you to travel 50 feet from a hotel to the highway running in front of it.

51

You should be aware that you may have a driver who has never been to the area that you are asking him or her to take you to. Your itinerary for the driver should have turn-by-turn instructions to help him and you stay on course.

To be sure, the driver can't be holding a piece of paper reading the instructions while he is driving. So, as the tour conductor, I always sit behind the driver and when we are close to a turn, unless I see his turn signal on, I give him a quiet reminder.

In the last few years, most drivers have a portable GPS on the dashboard and if you have given them an itinerary with addresses for restaurants, motels, etc. they often will have put the days' stops into the GPS in advance. This can be a tremendous help, but be aware, occasionally the GPS will tell you to turn right when actually you need to turn left.

Evaluating Hotels and Motels

When scouting a hotel, motel, attraction, etc. be sure to check access for a 45 foot, 12' 6" tall motorcoach. Overnight parking for the bus is another factor to check or ask about. If you're planning to use a hotel in the heart of a large city, often the parking will be in a pay lot or some distance from the hotel. The sales manager in the hotel will be able to tell you what they recommend.

Most major attractions expect buses and have made their roads and parking lots to accommodate them. However, if you are planning a tour that is "off the beaten path", make sure there aren't any "bus traps" that would be embarrassing with 40 to 50 passengers on the bus. A "bus trap" is a sharp turn with curbs or a dead-end driveway that would be difficult to turn around in.

Most hotels and motels will "comp" one room for every 20 paid rooms. "Comp" means the room is provided complimentary, in other words without charge to you. Sometimes you need to ask for a comp room if they don't readily offer one. Don't get too hung up on whether a hotel will give a comp room or not. If they won't offer a comp room, you must remember to add the cost of your room into the cost of the tour.

For example, if room and tax is $100 and you expect to have 40 people traveling with you, the additional cost of your room per person is only $2.50. This is not a reason to choose one hotel or motel over another. A few hotels and motels will also offer a special "driver's rate", which is usually a 50% discount.

Be sure to include all of the costs of housing yourself and the driver as well as any other charges or fees you are going to pay into the costs of the tour. These costs will be included in calculating the price for the tour and ultimately will be paid by your travelers.

When calling a hotel or motel to check on availability and rates, make sure you tell the sales manager or general manager that you are planning a tour to their area and are interested in bringing a group to their property. Ask all the questions that you haven't gotten answered from the Internet. A list of potential questions to ask the hotel representative follows:

- What is the best group rate you can provide for our date?
- What is the total room tax rate? (Don't ever forget this one)
- Do you often have groups staying with you?
- What is the age of your property? Has it been renovated lately?
- Is it your policy to comp one room for 20 paid rooms?
- Do you offer a special rate for the driver?
- Do you provide breakfast? Hot or cold?
- Can you provide luggage handling for a fee? What is the fee? If you don't normally, do you have someone who can do this?
- Do you provide parking for our bus?
- Do you have a restaurant and/or do you provide banquet catering?
- Ask them to send a banquet menu with price including tax and tip.
- If no restaurant, are there ones they could recommend for a group dinner?
- Finally, ask if they will comp a room for you for a site inspection? Make your inspection date on a weekday to improve your chances!

When you call with these questions, have a date in mind for your site inspection and a time that you would be available to meet with the GM or Sales Manager. The best time is usually the morning after you have stayed at their property. Often the manager will suggest meeting for breakfast. An early morning meeting will allow you to have more daylight for your scouting trip.

This meeting is a time to look over their group contract and see if there are any conditions that you would need to negotiate. Be especially aware of cancellation terms. If they have cancellation terms that begin more than 30 days in advance of your arrival, try to negotiate them down to 30 days.

.Sometimes you can't be sure that a tour will have enough travelers to make it profitable until about 45 days out, when you are ready to send out the requests for final payment. At that time, you should have the flexibility to cancel and not lose any deposits. Most motels and hotels will understand and agree to adjust their terms.

Often harsh cancellation terms of 60 or 90 days are in major city hotel contracts because they book large meetings and conventions where they hold dozens if not hundreds of rooms and must protect themselves from a cancellation of this magnitude. Remind them that you can only accommodate about 50 passengers on a bus so your room needs will be in the range of 25 to 30.

If your scouting trip does not allow time for you to stay in each hotel you have tentatively selected for your tour, make an appointment to stop and visit the property and meet the sales manager or general manager. Ask to see a couple of the rooms as well as the breakfast room, the restaurant, if any, and banquet rooms if you are planning a group dinner.

Ask about luggage service, often called "porterage" by hotel people. On our tours, we always provided luggage handling at each overnight stop. It's a service that people truly appreciate, and it's included in the price they pay. In many cases, especially when doing tours into more remote areas, we use motels that may not normally receive bus tours and don't have bellmen on staff.

If the motel normally doesn't offer luggage service, ask if they will have their maintenance staff do it or if they have teenage sons or daughters that would like to earn some extra money. I have had motels in Gallup, New Mexico, Moab, Utah, Green River, Utah and other remote places find a way to provide luggage handling in order to book a group of 25-30 rooms.

The charge for luggage handling roundtrip (in upon arrival, out upon departure) varies, but is usually from as low as $3.00 per bag to as high as $8.00 per bag. In a large city hotel, it may even be higher and sometimes is set by a union contract.

Almost all tour companies have a rule of just one large bag per person. The guests can also bring a carryon, but that is their responsibility and will not be handled by hotel/motel personnel. The carryon should not be a small suitcase, but rather a soft bag that can go in the overhead rack in the bus.

When scouting attractions such as museums, historical parks, theme parks, etc. along the way, it's wise to call ahead and ask questions about group rates, hours of operation, etc. Ask if they will comp your admission when you visit on your scouting trip. In almost all cases, an attraction will be happy to comp you if they feel like you aren't scamming them.

If you can give the attraction your website address, send them a letter or brochure or just be convincing on the phone they will most likely welcome you. If you are just starting your business and they are skeptical, you might tell them that you want to meet with them and take a quick walk around (30-45 minutes) to get a feel for the attraction. You are not there trying to see everything.

Make it clear that you are on a scouting trip for an upcoming tour and you are not on vacation. If all else fails and you feel that this attraction is a "must" for your tour, you might just have to cough up the money for an admission ticket or two and charge it to your scouting expense.

Keep Track of Scouting Expenses

Speaking of the expense of scouting a new tour; this expense is fully deductible as a business expense of your LLC or your corporation. I suggest you get a business credit card and charge everything you can to that card while on a scouting trip. The one exception, something that should not be charged to your business credit card, is your meals. Let me explain why.

The current tax law only allows you to deduct 50% of the actual cost of business meals when traveling. However, my accountant gave me a valuable tip many years ago that relieves you from the burden of keeping a diary of meal expenses along with actual receipts.

Every year the US government publishes a schedule of Per Diem expenses available on the Internet at www.gsa.gov/perdiem.

This per diem schedule is used by government employees when they are traveling and is fully accepted by the dreaded IRS. It includes lodging, which you won't use, but the right column has the approved daily costs for "Meals & Incidental Expenses", (often abbreviated as "M&IE" on the printouts).

To use the online schedule you enter the city and state or the ZIP code of where you will end each day on your scouting trip. The standard rate (this can change each October 1st) for meals and incidentals is currently $46 per person, per day, but in many areas it is higher, up to $71, and is intended to be a reflection of the actual cost of meals in various areas.

For instance, San Francisco and New York show a current rate of $71 and San Antonio has a rate of $66. If you are scouting with your spouse or a business partner, your actual expense will be 50% of the per diem rate times two ($46 x 2 x 50%) or $46. This calculation isn't really necessary since you can see that if you take the rate per person that will be the allowable rate for two.

The advantage of using the government's per diem rate is that the IRS can never challenge your claim for meal expenses (since it's their own figure) and you do not need to save receipts or keep a diary.

See Figure 5 in the Illustrations Section for an introduction to the various rates for Meals and Incidental Expenses (M&IE).

It is wise, however, to keep all your non-meal receipts and when you get back from the scouting trip, enter all the expenses for each day into an *Excel* worksheet or some other simple form to prove that your trip was for scouting purposes. You should sign and date each expense form.

See Figure 6 for a copy of one of my trip expense reports so you can prepare something similar for yourself.

Keep Good Notes on your Scouting Trip

Be sure to keep good notes on your scouting trip and list any concerns or questions you would need to have answered before you finalize the itinerary and the costs. As soon as possible after returning from your scouting trip, you should put together a detailed itinerary and cost spreadsheet for your prospective tour.

If you are planning a tour well into the future, you will have to estimate some costs. For instance, if your tour is 18 months in the future, hotels will give you a room rate quote, but some restaurants and hotel banquet personnel may be reluctant to guarantee a price for a group dinner. In that case, ask them to provide you a current banquet menu, pick the entrée that you would like for your guests and add two or three dollars in anticipation of a price increase.

If the price increase happens, you will likely be covered. If the prices stay the same, you have a few dollars extra profit or enough to cover some other price increase.

I can't emphasize enough that you need to ask hotels and restaurants to include their tax rate with their quote. Many times they won't include the total amount due because, like any retailer, they want you to focus on their price, not on the total including tax.

How to Charter a Bus

You probably have seen a big, beautiful bus traveling on the highway with the name of the tour company (Collette, Globus, Trafalger) clearly visible on the side. In almost all cases, that bus is chartered from a bus company and the tour company sign on the side is one that can be removed with a heat gun and changed to another tour company sign the next week.

In a few cases, if a major tour company does enough business in a certain area, they can request (demand) that the bus company have one or two buses in their fleet that have their tour company name permanently affixed. This way they are advertising their world-wide business while they are touring.

If, like me, you expect to operate a small tour company, one tour at a time, you aren't going to need this kind of bus-side advertising.

Why You Should <u>Never</u> Own a Bus

Purchasing a motorcoach is NOT something you want to consider if you intend to keep your business small, and in most cases, not even if your business gets very successful. Modern motorcoaches today cost at least $500,000 to purchase. If you are thinking of starting a tour business so that you can live your childhood dream of driving a big, beautiful motorcoach, buy several and start a charter bus company instead.

Imagine the monthly payment you would have with a $500,000 bus! On the other hand, don't even consider buying an older bus (for only a couple hundred thousand dollars) to get started. The cost of operating a bus is considerable and includes licensing, insurance, maintenance, plus paying a qualified and licensed driver.

The cost of owning a bus rather than chartering one when you have the need will take away from your tour profits and can bring on some major financial stress if the bus has a transmission or engine failure, or if you have to cancel one or more tours because your bus is in the shop.

When you charter from a company that has a fleet of buses, maintenance is their responsibility and you will be sheltered from those issues. Make sure the company has a fleet of buses, not just one or two, so that they can provide a "rescue" bus if you have problems on your tour.

If, on the other hand, a local bus company with only one or two buses is your best option, make sure you discuss with them their emergency procedures and agreements that they may have with other bus companies to assist them in a rescue situation. Don't wait until you are broken down along the side of the highway to ask about this!

A breakdown only happened to us one time in 19 years and 171 tours, but it can happen to anyone, and you must have a plan.

Bus charter companies can give you a quote in writing more than a year in advance. You can count on their quote. They will provide a clean, comfortable bus with an experienced driver because they want to keep your business. The tour business and the bus business are two very different enterprises and, in my opinion, should not be mixed.

I don't know of a major, nation-wide tour company that owns buses.

Here's another reason for not owning a bus: If you decide to offer tours that require a flight to the tour starting point several hundred or several thousand miles from your location, you can charter a bus for that "transfer" (a move of your group to an airport or pier where you will use another form of transportation to continue on).

When you reach the airport or the cruise terminal, you release the bus and driver and he begins his trip back to his home base. If you own a bus, and especially if you intend to drive your own bus, where do you leave it while you are touring or cruising? In fact, your vehicle will be sitting without earning its keep while you are worrying about it and your group is touring or cruising.

I think you can get the idea that I don't think buying a bus, new or used, is a good idea for a tour company.

Selecting a Charter Bus Company

Before you can price your first tours, you are going to need to know what a bus from a good quality bus charter company is going to cost you. To select a charter bus company, I recommend you make arrangements with their charter sales department to visit their yard and look at the age and appearance of their buses, the quality of their maintenance facilities and the willingness of their staff to work with you as you begin your business.

Questions to ask should include their policy for "rescue" of you and your group in case of a bus failure en route. Do they have 24-hour dispatch to help you in case of an emergency situation and do they have reciprocal agreements with other bus companies to help out in case they have no buses or drivers available to send? A bus breakdown is very rare, but it can happen and you need to know how they will respond in such a situation.

If you intend to operate quality tours, you are going to need quality buses. Ask the age of their fleet and check to see if the company has a program to replace buses on a regular basis. Many bus charter companies will replace their buses as they age because the larger tour companies demand that any bus they charter be less than five years old.

As a small tour operator, you may not be in a position to demand the charter company's newest buses but my experience is that if you foster a positive relationship with your charter companies, they will be sure to give you quality buses plus good and personable drivers.

To allow the bus company to quote you a price or give you a bid for a prospective tour, you need to tell them where you expect the bus to travel each day. At this point they don't need to know every stop and every turn you're going to make, but you need to have a general outline of where you'll be going.

A simple request for quote could look like this:

Mon	Oct 13	Bus deadhead Phoenix to Lake Havasu City
Tue	Oct 14	Lake Havasu to Sedona, AZ
Wed	Oct 15	Sedona to Flagstaff
Thu	Oct 16	Flagstaff to Lake Havasu City
		Bus will deadhead back to Phoenix

In most cases, the above itinerary gives the bus company enough information to calculate mileage and quote a rate for this 3-day tour. Make sure that the quote you receive includes taxes and fuel surcharges, if any.

If you are requesting a quote for a tour a year or more in the future, the company may quote "subject to fuel surcharges". If so, ask for their policy on fuel surcharges. For instance, they should be able to tell you that fuel surcharges will be added if the price of diesel fuel exceeds a certain figure. This is reasonable, since they can't determine a year or more in advance what the cost of fuel might be.

For you to be able to handle an increase in cost after you have put out your schedule with prices, means that you must state somewhere in your brochure and/or detailed itinerary for a tour or cruise, that "fuel surcharges, if any, will be added to the final invoice".

If you have the availability of several bus companies within a reasonable distance from your town, I would suggest visiting more than one and request quotes from each one. If the quotes are significantly different, you should ask the sales manager at each company to explain why they are higher or lower than their competition.

Remember that you are the customer and they should be anxious to get your business, so if they have difficulty answering you or treat you like you shouldn't be questioning their quotes, they may not be the company you want to choose.

A final point about your transportation choices: For your very first tours, until you have established yourself in your town, you may have to take a few small groups of 5 to 15 people. The cost of a bus for a small size group is prohibitive. However, rather than cancel a tour, consider renting a 7 or 15 passenger van and driving the tour yourself.

Taking a small group certainly limits your profit opportunity, but it gets you started and, as it did with our business, it got us off the ground during our first year. Our first five tours ranged in passenger count from 3 to 12. We lost a little money on the tour with just 3 people, but we gained experience and we didn't disappoint those three people.

Most charter bus companies have smaller buses, usually in the 24 to 32 seat range. These buses generally do not have a restroom, but are a less expensive alternative for a mid-size group. The relative cost is usually about 75% of the cost of a full-size 56 passenger bus and they come with a fully qualified and licensed driver.

As far as pricing at the beginning of your tour business, I would price based on a reasonable profit for a mid-size group of 20-25. If you have fewer, you generally can still break even or make a very small profit.

However, if you are pleasantly surprised when you have excellent response to your offering and have a higher passenger count, consider adjusting your price downward in your letter requesting final payment. Explain in your letter that due to

63

the great response to your tour, you are able to reduce the price. People don't see that happen very often and it will buy a lot of loyalty!

Any of your travelers who receive a lower final invoice than expected will be certain to tell their friends and neighbors about you. This has a positive effect on your local reputation and will go a long way toward building your business.

Calculating the Price for a Tour

Calculating the price for each tour is critical to the success of your tour and your business. It must be done accurately and thoroughly before you publish the price in your brochure, online or in an advertisement. It's bad business practice, and certainly embarrassing, if you have taken reservations and then find that you have priced the tour at less than it will cost you to operate it.

Using a Spreadsheet Program

The use of a spreadsheet program like Microsoft *Excel* is highly advised. *Excel* is one of the products you purchase within Microsoft Office. If you've never used a computer spreadsheet you can find tutorials on line by using a search engine such as Google.

An *Excel* spreadsheet is made up of a page with rows and columns. The rows are always numbered starting with "1" at the top and the columns start with "A" at the left. You enter figures or make calculations in "cells". The first cell at the left top is "A1".

For a simple example, think of an invoice where you are selling two shovels at a price of $12.00 each. The left-most column "A" would be for quantity; the next column to the right, "B" would have a description of the item, Column "C" would be for price and the fourth column, "D" would be for amount.

Let's assume the invoice has lines for company name and address and the first line on your *Excel* sheet is line "5". So, in cell A5 you would enter the quantity "2". Tabbing once (or moving with the right arrow key) to the right on the same line, you would enter description, "shovel" into cell B5; then tabbing once again, enter the price of "12.00" into cell C5. The amount will be calculated in cell D5 by entering this formula: =A5*C5 and hitting enter.

Excel will make the calculation in the blink of your eye. This is just a very simple example of using a spreadsheet but I cannot emphasize enough the necessity for you to learn and utilize a spreadsheet program in your tour business.

If you have not used *Excel* before, search on Google or another search engine for "Excel tutorials" and then select one for the year of your *Excel* (i.e. Excel 2010). Just an hour or two with a tutorial and you will be able to do most of the spreadsheets necessary for your tour business.

See Figure 7 for an example of my spreadsheet for a simple 3-day, 2-night tour to Death Valley, California.

Your spreadsheets for a tour will be quite simple to design. To begin, just follow my sample spreadsheet in laying out your own spreadsheets.

Begin your spreadsheet on Line 1, Column A by typing the tour name. Type the date on Line 3, Column A under the tour name. Then going across to the right, type in Columns B, C and D, "Per Person", "Total", and "Single" in that order. In Row 4, under "Per Person" enter the number of travelers you are planning on carrying and copy or enter that same number into the same row under "Total".

Since the rest of the spreadsheet will be showing dollars and cents, highlight columns B, C and D under what you have already entered by starting in B6, holding down the left button on your mouse and going across to D6 then down to the bottom of the page, still highlighting only the three columns.

Release the left mouse button (the three columns will remain highlighted) then go to the middle of the upper banner to the "Number" box and click on the down arrow right of "General" and click on "Number". Now, if you enter 12 into a cell in row 6 or below, *Excel* will display it as "12.00".

Enter "Day 1" and the date in cell A5 and begin listing expenses in column A beginning in A6.

The first expense items to list are those that are "fixed" such as, the bus charter, an overnight room for the driver before the tour, if necessary, snacks, water and other items that you won't be charging per person. Then, using your day-by-day itinerary as a guide, enter into the left column (Column A) of your spreadsheet all the expenses in order for Day 1.

List all costs of the tour that you intend to provide; any morning attractions, lunch (if you are providing it), any afternoon attractions, lodging cost, luggage handling, dinner, etc. for the first day of the tour. Make sure all of your expenses include the taxes that you will be charged and tips that may not be included. Next, go on to Day 2, Day 3, etc. listing each expense type in Column A.

In Column B enter any amounts that are provided to you by individual, like meals, admissions, luggage handling, etc. In Column C, enter those items where you have a single cost for the tour, such as the bus charter, snacks and water that you may be providing, cost for a parking lot rental, if any, etc.

For the smaller items, such as a lunch, you may not know the actual figure a year in advance so it is appropriate to enter an estimate. Make this a dollar or two higher than you think it will be so it doesn't end up coming out of your pocket.

After you've entered a cost for each item in Column B or C, enter the calculations necessary in Columns B, C & D. For instance, you've entered a figure for the bus charter in Column C. You want the per-person cost in Column B and D. So, with your cursor in Column B on the same row, enter an equals sign (=), click on the bus cost in C5, enter a forward slash "/" (for division) then click on the number of travelers in B5 and hit enter. Then do the same thing for Column D.

It may take several days to make the contacts with motels, restaurants and attractions to get your costs. As you get the individual costs in writing, enter each into the spreadsheet. Over time, the spreadsheet will fill in and you will have an accurate estimate of your costs.

Pricing to Make a Profit

When you have completed adding in all costs for the planned tour, it's time to determine the price that you are going to charge. For you to get to go "free" is not reason enough to have a tour business – that's called a "hobby". So, in addition to including any costs for yourself that are not already covered, you need to decide what to add as a reasonable profit.

Of course, this also depends on the number of travelers you expect will want to go with you. If you are just starting out, you may be forced to do as we did by taking our first five tours in 1993 in a rented 15-passenger van with both my wife and I driving. By the way, this is perfectly legal in Arizona and most states without a Commercial Drivers License (CDL) if there are 15 or fewer passengers.

As you can imagine, our profit on that first tour was low – about $300 – but we gained invaluable experience. In fact, those people on our early van tours continued to travel with us for years and were instrumental in getting the word out about Bartlett Tours. I would recommend you do the same thing with your first few tours, if necessary, to get the word out and build a following.

After your first few tours, and in a smaller community, (ours was 22,000 when we started in 1993 but has grown to about 52,000) the word will get around quickly if your first travelers come home satisfied and ready to go on another tour with you.

For pricing purposes, I would suggest using a conservative number of 25-30 participants for your beginning tours. I would also suggest that you offer short tours of 1, 2 or 3 days at the beginning to give people a chance to try your tours without spending a lot of money. This also makes it easier to gain the experience you need with real paying passengers in the seats.

Most costs on a tour are per-person costs and go up with the number of travelers (rooms, meals, admissions, etc.). But one of the major costs, the bus charter, stays the same no matter how many people are traveling, so the cost per person for the bus goes down the more people you have.

Remember, however, with smaller groups, that very few hotels or motels will comp a room for you if you have fewer than 20 "paid for" rooms, so this will increase your costs slightly.

On an overnight tour to Palm Springs that we conducted in February, 2012, and priced at $319 per person, double occupancy, my spreadsheet program showed that if I took 30 people, the net profit would be $1,770; if I took 40 people, the net profit would be $3,546 or twice the profit by adding just 10 people.

But, if we took 48 people, as we actually did, the net profit was $4,967, or nearly three times the profit earned with only 30 people. The bus charter cost for this tour was $3,250. This illustrates that spending a few hundred dollars on some advertising to increase the number of participants can pay off handsomely.

See Figures 8, 9 and 10 for a spreadsheet illustration of this pricing effect with 30, 40 and 48 passengers. Notice the change in per-person cost of the bus charter.

The way I priced a tour was by deciding how much profit I would like to make per person or per day. After our five van tours, when I started taking groups of 40 to 50 passengers on tours that we had designed and scouted, I decided I wanted to make at least $800 to $1,000 per day. As we got more successful in the following years, I increased the minimum profit to about $1,500 per day. Due to the high number of travelers on many of our tours, we often cleared $2,000 or more per day.

So, by using my computer spreadsheet, I would total all per-passenger expenses then add enough to the cost to make my intended profit. This isn't very scientific, but then it doesn't need to be. What you want to do is offer a high quality product (your tour) at a reasonable price and make a reasonable profit.

Profit from a Major Tour or Cruise

In the case of tours that I have contracted for with a larger firm, I have always been satisfied with a somewhat smaller profit. I was willing to do this because I didn't have to incur the cost of scouting the tour, making all the arrangements with individual hotels, restaurants, attractions, etc., so my effort expended was less.

For example, if I were contracting with Collette Vacations for a 9-day "New England Fall Color" tour, as we did in 2010, I would use my spreadsheet to add up all the expenses, using 40 guests for planning purposes, and then I would plug in different prices until I came up with about $1,200 to $1,500 profit per day.

If the tour were to sell well, as this one did, and I was able to take more than 40 people, the profit would be significantly better. In fact, we took 48 travelers on the New England 2010 tour and netted $1,726 per day for a net profit of $15,534!

The same is true when you take your guests on a cruise. The work is pretty easy once you get your travelers on the ship and a profit of $1,000 to $1,500 per day, $7,000 to $10,500 for a 7-day cruise, is well worth your while. I'll talk more about cruises later.

Be aware that in your pricing, you should always try to price your product like retail stores and auto dealers do. In other words, when using a factor such as I've mentioned in the last few paragraphs and it indicates a price of $305, consider lowering the price to $295 or $299.

If $305 is the lowest possible price you can come up with, you might as well go up to $319 and make a little extra profit since my experience has shown that at this point the price is already over a "threshold" and a little extra won't affect sales of the tour.

Getting Quotes for Hotels & Motels

When getting quotes for lodging, attractions and other elements of a tour, don't forget to ask for their "comp" policy. Again, a comp (short for complimentary) is when a vendor such as a hotel or motel, offers you a free room if you have more than a certain number of paid rooms.

A common ratio for a comp room is one comp for at least 20 paid rooms. This room is no different from the other rooms you will be utilizing and it doesn't matter who gets the "free" room. In fact, there is no free room.

It works this way: if all your rooms are $100 plus 12% tax and you are occupying a total of 23 rooms, you should be charged for only 22, saving you $112.00. This needs to be on the contract the hotel/motel sends you, so be sure you watch for it. If it isn't on there, talk to the sales manager and ask that they send another contract with that comp policy shown.

When paying for lodging, either in advance or upon check-out, be sure to check the statement and count the rooms you are being charged for. Often, the front desk is not aware that there should be a comp room and will charge for all rooms. It's always easier to get the bill corrected before you pay than try to get it corrected later.

In calculating the price for a tour, I always use the comp room for my wife and me by not including a room charge for us. On the other hand, if you are staying at a hotel that does not offer a comp room; don't forget to add into your costs the cost of your own room. You want your travelers to pay for your room since they are paying for you to escort or guide the tour.

If the best the hotel will offer is one comp for every 25 paid rooms, (this is often true if the hotel is a large city convention hotel and is used to large groups), it makes it very difficult for a bus tour to have enough paid rooms to earn the one comp room.

To earn a comp room, you would have to have 50 travelers with double occupancy (two to a room), or slightly less if you have a few singles (for example, 23 double occupancy rooms plus two single occupancy rooms). Your room, as escort, would then be the 26th room and would be comped. Even at that, a last-minute cancellation of one room would cost you the comp room.

Never be afraid to challenge the number of paid rooms to qualify for a comp. Explain to the sales manager at the hotel that 25 paid rooms is almost unattainable and that you would prefer a comp at 20 paid rooms. My experience is that they will usually change that in the contract if you ask or they will allow you to line out "25" and enter "20" in that space and then initial the change.

Remember, in most cases, the hotel sales manager really wants your business now and in the future, so they don't want to lose you over a comp room issue.

A few hotels and motels will offer a special "driver rate". If they do, the price is often 50% of the regular rate plus tax. This will be in addition to one comp room, but in my experience it is rare that the driver rate is offered. It never hurts to ask when you are negotiating the contract with the hotel.

What if you are pricing two hotels in the same area and the rates are comparable but one offers a comp room and the other does not? First of all, I would talk with the sales manager or general manager and make it clear that you are comparing the two proposals and let him know that a comp room is important in your decision.

However, if you really prefer the accommodations or location of the one that is not giving a comp, I would go with the better accommodations. In using the room pricing from above, $112 additional cost divided by 45 travelers causes only a $2.49 per person difference in cost. The "wow" factor of really good accommodations is worth a lot more than that.

Advertising and Promoting Your Tours

No business can be successful if people, known as customers, don't know the business exists. It is your responsibility to make your city, town or area, know that you exist and that you bring them something special. Travel can often be the highlight of life for people who enjoy a little adventure and change in their lives.

You need to understand that the major audience for group tours is the older, retired generation. This is because they have the two necessary ingredients: time and money. This isn't to say that everyone who has reached the "golden years" has the money, but those who have planned for retirement often have the money and are looking for new and exciting experiences.

Going with a group on a tour for many people is a safe way to see the world. Many older people are afraid of traveling alone, even as couples, and will look at a group tour as a way to travel in a safe and secure manner. Safety is important, but the anticipation and expectation of having fun with a group from the same area is always more important in making the decision to go with you.

If you are just starting your business, often the local newspaper will do a feature story on the new business that is starting up in town. Go to the newspaper office and talk with the feature editor with a prepared story or outline about your new tour business.

Watch for other similar stories and use those as a template for what to write about your business. Be sure, they will change your story but they will appreciate that you have done some of the work for them and they're more likely to run it. Make sure they understand that you are also going to buy advertising with the paper.

The Importance of a Logo

"logo" – a distinctive symbol, sign or emblem adopted by a business or organization to identify the overall company, its products, uniform, vehicles, etc. A logo identifies a business in its simplest form via the use of a mark or icon.

A logo is a simple name or symbol that immediately identifies the business to someone seeing an advertisement or other visual. Think of the logos of McDonald's, Chevrolet or Nike, and they immediately come to mind.

Although your logo doesn't need to be fancy or too clever, a logo is important to use in your advertising for consistency and for instant recognition. My logo was simply "Bartlett Tours" shown in a distinctive way:

This simple logo was used in all my advertising and promotion for the 19 years we were in business (with the exception of the "article type" ads as shown in Figure 12). When we sold the business in 2012, the new owners purchased this logo and continued its use because it was so well known in our city.

I encourage you to develop a logo of your company name that will help your business get known quickly. If you don't think you can come up with something, ask friends if they know a graphic artist or an art student in high school who could come up with several designs for you to choose from.

A logo should be simple and easy to identify, so don't let someone assisting you get to clever in the design.

A couple of years into our business, I came up with a "tag line" to use in our advertising and promotion. The tag line was:

"With Bartlett Tours, it's the experience"

Or, sometimes simply,

"It's the experience"

Naturally, when I came up with the tag line, I was meaning that when someone went on a Bartlett Tour, they would not only enjoy the travel and the camaraderie of the other travelers on the tour, but they would come away happy with the overall experience. This was most oftentimes the result.

But later, it became evident that even if something went wrong on a tour, it was still part of the "experience".

In 2001 our group arrived at the airport in Milan for our return flight from a tour of Italy to be informed that our flight would be delayed several hours due to a bird hitting and breaking the windshield on our plane. I informed my travelers of the delay and we all began our wait.

Sometime during the 7-hour wait, a woman who was traveling with us walked by where my wife and I were sitting and said with a smile, "it's the experience". Everyone in the group sitting around us had a good laugh and I realized that the tag line worked both ways. Often you remember the little set-backs in life as well as you remember all the things that went right.

Somewhere on most letters, brochures and other communication with my travelers, I found a way to end with, "Remember, with Bartlett Tours, it's the experience".

Newspaper Advertising

Newspaper advertising is the most common form of advertising and it works well for a tour business. Small, repetitive ads in a local paper make people aware that you exist. Your ad should lead them to call for more information. When they call, you will have a chance to ask their name and address, plus email address if they have one, for follow-up information.

See Figure 11 and Figure 12 in the Illustrations Section for examples of my newspaper ads.

You will see that we did both regular display ads and we did ads that looked more like articles about an upcoming tour. Overall, it seemed we got better response from the ads that looked like a news article and provided more detail about a particular tour.

If you are in a remote area, advertising in the local newspaper is probably one of your best values. I found that smaller, repetitive ads attracted more inquiries than large, occasional ads. You will want some of the ads to promote the next eight or ten tours with only their tour title, while other ads should concentrate on only one tour and give a description of the tour with the highlights and of course, the dates.

Although I usually included the tour price in my single-tour ads, I occasionally left the price out of the ad in hopes that people would call to check on price and I could get them on my mailing list. I was never quite sure which way worked best.

My local newspaper ad representative would occasionally call and offer a large one-time ad at a very attractive price. Often this ad was in color. The catch was that she would need the ad to her within a few hours. These ads are known as "space available" and are offered at a low rate and on short notice to fill an open spot in the newspaper. These ads are great values if you can get them.

See Figure 13 for an example of a larger "space available" ad that we ran.

If you get to know the feature editor at your newspaper, he or she may be willing to do a story about something interesting that you have done. In 2001, I considered offering a river cruise the next year from Moscow to St Petersburg, Russia, a 15-day excursion.

My wife and I went on the Russia River cruise in June, 2001 to scout it and be sure it was something we wanted to offer. It was a cruise with about 120 Americans on board a luxurious river boat. We thoroughly enjoyed the experience and found the Russian people at our ports of call very friendly and welcoming.

When we returned home, I contacted the feature editor of our local newspaper and after a two-hour interview; she printed our story on the front page of the second section of the Sunday newspaper with several photographs, all in color! There was no charge for this because it was news! It was certainly a great promotion for our tours.

Unfortunately, just three months later, on September 11, 2001, the World Trade Center was attacked and both towers were destroyed. After that terrible tragedy, and the warning of other attacks to come, we cancelled all tours that involved flying for 2002 and, for whatever reason; we never got back to offering the Russia river cruise again.

Ads in Local Live Theatre Programs

If your community has a local live theatre or a community concert association, ads in their programs hit right at your target audience. These venues attract a high percentage of retirees who are candidates for your tour offerings. One ad is usually kept in the brochure for the duration of their theatre season and can often be a very good value.

See Figure 14 for a sample of an ad in a live theatre program and Figure 15 for an ad that we ran in a local arts guide.

A Tour Brochure

Before you conduct your first tour, you should develop a tour brochure. At the beginning, your brochure can be quite simple, maybe listing only a few tours that you plan to offer. But, no matter how simple, it needs to look professional. If this is not something you feel capable of designing, using Microsoft *Publisher* or something similar, ask around your town and see who might be able to do it for you.

The brochure should highlight the name you have given to your business, a small editorial-type article stating that you are just starting your tour business and would appreciate everyone spreading the news. In addition, your prospective travelers will want to know something about you and why you are now beginning a tour business.

A good reason to give for starting a tour business is that you have always enjoyed traveling and now want to provide a service for your area that makes traveling to exciting and interesting places available to more people. Emphasize that you are a local business and that all your tours will be leaving from a location in town.

Of course, you want to have a title line for each tour that shows the date, the name of the tour and the price. The price for a tour is always shown as the price per person, double occupancy, sometimes shown as "ppdo". Double occupancy means that if you have priced your tour at $495, that price is for each person sharing the room with another who is usually a spouse or a friend.

You can also show the single occupancy price somewhere in the description. You will need to be able to answer to people why you charge more for a single person, because some people see it as a penalty. It is not a penalty! It is because all hotel and motel rooms are priced for up to two persons whether there is one person or two actually using the room.

I usually use an illustration to explain this concept. If someone is going alone to an out-of-town concert or conference, and the rooms are $100 per night, they will pay $100. But, if they have a friend going to the same event, and they decide to share, they will only pay $50 per person. That seems to make sense and it usually helps them understand that it is not a penalty.

Of course, the body of the paragraph promoting a single tour should be the description written in a way that makes the tour sound so interesting and fun that they want to call and ask some questions. Make sure you emphasize the exciting and fun parts of each tour in your brochure.

The last line of the tour description should be what is included in the price. Most likely this will include transportation, the number of nights lodging, all admissions, the number of breakfasts, lunches and dinners provided.

As you begin to advertise, you will need a brochure of your tours available to mail or email to every person that calls. As you get calls and record them in your customer record system, you are building a base of potential customers. These names will become your mailing list from then on. If you are friends with business or professional people in town, you can ask them if they would be willing to have your brochure displayed in their office or waiting room.

A brochure must look professional and must create an excitement and a "sense of urgency" about each tour. You want the reader to feel that they need to call now before the tour is sold out. You also want them to get the feeling that your tours are <u>fun</u> as well as interesting.

See Figure 16 for a copy of one of my 4-page brochures.

Producing and Mailing a Tour Brochure

I began work on my next brochure about two to three months before I wanted to have it ready for the printer. Using Microsoft *Publisher*, and using a layout that I had developed in the early years of my business, I began writing the description of each tour. If I didn't have a final price available for that tour, I would put "$XX" in place of the price as a reminder to fill it in before sending it to the printer.

After I was reasonably sure everything was correct, I had my wife proofread my work for errors in spelling, punctuation, and readability. If she had a problem understanding what I meant with something, it was sure to be something that our travelers would have trouble understanding. I would then rewrite the sentence to make it easier to understand.

When everything seemed to be correct, I sent my final digital files to a local printer who added our picture, which I provided, then added a new color that I picked for this issue of the brochure. They then provided a "proof" in about a week, that I read carefully and sometimes with minor changes, I approved. The printing and folding took about another week.

I chose to have my brochures printed on glossy, 80 pound, 11" x 17" paper. This heavier paper not only looked more professional but it was sturdier and made it through the mail sorting equipment with very little trouble. The printer would fold the paper twice, making the size for mailing 8 ½" x 5 ½".

As soon as the printer had our brochures completed, my wife and I worked hard to get them in the mail the next day. I printed the address labels using Lotus *Approach*. *Approach* allowed me to select those that I mailed to based on year of first inquiry or date of last tour. If someone had been getting our brochures for three years and had never traveled with us, I considered that they were no longer a good prospect.

In like manner, if someone had traveled with us, but had not traveled with us in the last three years, I considered that they were no longer able or no longer interested in traveling with us. Occasionally, I would get a call from a past traveler saying they hadn't gotten our new brochure. In that case, I would explain why and quickly mail them a brochure.

These decisions were made at the time I used *Approach* to find the records and before printing the mailing labels.

As I put labels on the new brochures, I occasionally looked at the name and remembered that they had move away recently or that they had a change in their life. In this case, I passed on sending them the brochure and updated my record.

With me putting the address labels on and my wife putting the stamps on, we could do 1,000 brochures in about six hours.

A note about the picture we used on each brochure. We chose to use a different picture on each brochure. Because we were generally on at least one ocean cruise each year, and cruises always have photographers on board, we asked the photographer to take several portrait-type photos of us from the chest up. We would then buy one or more of these photos at $20 each for use on a future brochure.

Occasionally, I had extra space in a brochure, so I filled the space by including one or two small pictures of our destinations. For instance, if we were doing a tour to Durango and riding the Durango-Silverton steam train, I would include a picture of the locomotive. If the tour highlight was the Ronald Reagan Presidential Library, I would include a picture of President Reagan.

We mailed two brochures a year, in early October and early February. Since roughly half of our travelers were winter residents, I kept a summer and a winter address in my customer records. If I had a summer address outside of Lake Havasu City, I mailed our early October brochure to their home in Minnesota or wherever they spent the summer. Of course, if I had no summer address, I mailed to their local address.

Even though I mailed 800-1000 brochures each mailing, I did not use bulk mail. Bulk mail rates are lower than first class but the mail is not forwarded and if there has been an address change, you are not notified. Undelivered bulk mail goes directly into the trash. Since you have no notification, you will continue to mail to the incorrect address and your brochure continues to go into the trash.

The brochures mailed in February were all mailed to addresses in town. Although there were only minor changes between the October and February brochures, I wanted to remind my "snowbird" travelers to make reservations with us for the next winter before they left us for the summer.

Our "snowbird" season was from October through March, although some just came for January through March.

A Website for your Tour Business

In 19 years of operating my tour business (1993-2012), I watched a big change in the number of seniors that became computer users. In the last few years, I tried to collect as many email addresses as possible and would occasionally send out email "alerts" with last minute openings on a tour.

I also sent an email announcing an update to our tour schedule available on our website. In future years, I can see more promotion being done by email as well as Facebook and Twitter.

In today's environment, it is a "must" to have a website for your business. Many people prefer to go to a website to learn about your company rather than calling. The website also projects an image that you are keeping up with technology and are a sound and professional organization.

My website had the following sections:

Home Page: Welcome to the website, what we provide, a short history, our pledge of high quality, competence, safe travel

About Us: Our picture, our experience, a short history of the business

Tours: Detailed descriptions of each tour with dates and prices

FAQ's: A list of frequently asked questions

Contact Us: Phone, email and US Mail address

Insurance: A link to the Travel Guard Insurance website

See Figure 1, referenced earlier, to look at the sections of my website.

Unfortunately, when we sold our business, I didn't think about capturing the latest version of our website. Naturally, the new owners of our business wanted to change it to reflect the change in ownership.

By the time I thought about writing this book and including screenshots of our web pages, the changes had been made. My webmaster had a copy of the website as of 2007 and that is the best we could find. So, even though the pages of our 2012 website would have the same look, the details in the written portion are dated.

There are various ways to develop a website. My website was developed by a high school friend and resided on the free space given by my Internet Service Provider (ISP). Of course, you can spend some serious money and have a website developed by a professional team, but you may find a friend or a high school student in your town that would be happy to earn a few extra dollars by developing your site.

Whatever method you use, you need to come up with the content and then let them go about doing the technical work.

In 2013, there are several websites from which you can develop your own tour business website, if you have an interest in doing it yourself. The advantage of doing it yourself is that you develop the skill and the knowhow to be able to quickly update the website when you need to.

The disadvantage of doing it yourself is it may take some valuable time away from developing your tour business and delay the point at which you have revenue flowing in. Of course, if you are a novice at working with computers, I would highly recommend that you find someone with experience to do it for you.

There is no physical size limitation to a website like there is in a printed brochure. You can feel free to add pictures to each tour description, be as wordy as you want without feeling like you are going to run out of space. Be sure to have your own pictures on your website so that people can see what you look like and hopefully, decide that they would like to travel with you.

It's quite easy today to add video to a tour description or to your welcoming message. This can be video that you take with your own video camera or video of a destination that you find on YouTube. Video can add motion and excitement to your website that is not possible with your printed brochure.

Local Promotion Opportunities

Every club in town wants to have a good speaker or program for their members. If you have a hobby or special interest that would provide a program for local clubs and organizations, by all means, send letters to the various clubs and let them know you are available to speak at one of their meetings.

Of course, this means you've got to sit down and put together an interesting 15-20 minute talk. If your hobby is making jewelry, develop a talk about how to make jewelry and take your work to show. If you love to hike, take pictures of some of the places you've hiked and develop a slide show.

If you've rebuilt an old car or hotrod, tell about the challenges you faced in completing the project. Of course, a spouse could be the one giving these talks and promoting your joint business.

At the end of your program, take the opportunity to tell a little about your new business and your upcoming tours. Bring brochures and make them available. The people at the meeting will begin to tell others in town about your tours and your interesting talk and this activity will promote your tours.

Lake Havasu City is on the banks of the Colorado River. Before we moved here, I became aware that steamboats had traveled the Colorado from 1852 to 1916, carrying Army troops and supplies and ore from mines along the river. I did some research, copied some pictures onto slides, wrote a script and sent out letters. The first year we were in operation, 1993, I gave my "Steamboats on the Colorado River" talk at least 15 times.

When new people called, I would always ask, "Where did you hear about us"? Often I would hear that they were a member of some local club and were in the audience when I talked about steamboats. I continue to give the same talk today, 21 years later. But, since I no longer have a business to promote, I don't try to "sell" my free talk like I used to.

If your town has a street fair once or twice a year that draws people from the surrounding area, check into having a booth to meet people and hand out your brochures. Talking with people puts a face and a voice onto the brochure that you hand them and doubles the value.

If you have a radio station or a TV station in your area that does local interviews, make contact with them and see if they will interview you about your new business offering. The audience for local radio and TV stations is predominantly people who are retired and have the time to listen.

Advertising in a weekly or monthly shopper does not seem to be effective. Most people don't pick up a shopper unless they are looking for something – a car, a boat or a specific service. This type of advertising can be rather expensive and, in my experience, brings very limited results.

There are many avenues for advertising and promotion. Try all of them over time and weed out the ones that don't seem to work. The main objective is to get your company name out there and get people talking about your tours. This activity will promote interest that will translate into customers and profit for your tour business.

Conducting Your Own Tours

When you conduct your own tours, you are the host, the guide, the information center, the complaint department and the arbitrator. To your return guests, you will be a friend and fellow traveler. To the first-time guest, you are an unknown. Your job is to make everyone feel comfortable and welcome from the moment you meet them.

Preparing for Your Tour

Confirming Details of the Tour to Your Travelers

About 60-45 days before the tour, you will need to send a confirmation to each of your travelers. This letter confirms that they are booked on the tour, that you have received their deposit, and that final payment is due by a certain date. It also gives them sufficient information about the tour to eliminate any worry and lessen the possibility of multiple phone calls with questions.

This can be an invoice, but I preferred to send a letter which I believed was much more friendly and personal.

On the reverse side of the letter, I included the itinerary of the tour to get them excited about going and to reduce the number of phone calls asking about times and places we were going to visit.

See Figure 17 for a copy of a Confirmation Letter.

See Figure 18 for a copy of the Guest Itinerary.

I always included a return envelope for their convenience. I used a #9 return envelope which I stamped with Bartlett Tours and our address. This #9 envelope went into our printed #10 envelopes without folding. I sincerely believe that if there is an envelope included, the payment comes back quicker than if you leave it up to your customers to find their own envelope.

Information Forms

For those going on their first tour with us, I included with the Confirmation Letter a blank Information Form for each person to fill out.

See Figure 19 for a copy of the Information Form.

A completed Information Form for each guest was carried in my briefcase on every tour. It was generally only used if a person injured themselves or fell sick and it was necessary to call 911 for assistance. However, this form can also help the paramedics fill out their forms because sometimes a person is in pain and unable to answer questions.

The Information Form also gave the traveler's emergency contact name and phone number so that in the very few cases where we had to leave the person behind in the hospital, we were able to notify a relative or friend who could come to be with them or at least monitor the situation until they could arrange to get them home.

In between tours, I kept all the Information Forms from various tours in manila folders in loose alphabetical order. My first file was A-C; the second was D-F; etc. Before I sent the confirmation letter, I went through the files and pulled the forms for anyone who had traveled with us before. I checked the date of the form, because it was my policy to have them fill out a new form if the old form was over two years old.

In two years there could be health changes, emergency contact changes, etc. and if I needed the form for an emergency, (as I did in a number of cases) I wanted to be reasonably sure that the information on the form was accurate. If the form was outdated, I included a blank form with the confirmation letter and a small 1/3 page slip explaining why I was asking for a new form.

Terms and Conditions

If this was the first tour for this traveler, I also included a copy of our Terms and Conditions.

See Figure 20 for a copy of our Terms and Conditions.

It is very important that you send your terms and conditions to each traveler before their first tour with you. In fact, if you noticed near the bottom of the Information Form that I send out on the first tour, it states, *"I have received a copy of Bartlett Tours' Terms and Conditions and understand how they pertain to my participation in any part of this or future tour programs."*

You may notice also the paragraph stating, *"Bartlett Tours reserves the right at any time to dismiss anyone from the tour whose conduct has become injurious to the welfare and pleasure of other tour participants. The dismissed person must make their own arrangements for return home at their expense. No tour refund will be made"*.

Dealing with Disruptive Travelers

On only about three occasions, I had someone who was a negative person and was trying to spread negativity among the group. Usually, one of my loyal travelers would make me aware of the problem.

I would then approach the person who was complaining and say that I suspected something was wrong and I wanted him/her to tell me what the matter was. Usually they were embarrassed, but I told them I wanted them to be happy and if there was a problem, I wanted to try to fix it.

Generally the complainer would down-play the problem while talking with me. After listening, if there was anything I could actually do to improve the situation, I promised that I would. If not, I asked them to please forget the negativity and try to be positive so that it didn't take away from the enjoyment of others. Just the fact that I talked with them made the situation better in their mind and their attitude improved.

I only had one occasion to dismiss someone from a tour. A lady and her elderly mother were traveling on their first tour with us, a trip to Mesa Verde National Park, Durango and other points of interest in Southern Colorado. The information we sent out in advance noted that the tour required a moderate amount of walking.

I noticed at our first rest stop that they both had trouble walking and were very slow getting up the steps into the bus. It was literally taking two or three minutes for them to get into the bus and this was holding up the group.

The first evening, in a hotel in Gallup, New Mexico, the lady yelled across the dining room to me that their room was totally unacceptable and that they needed a handicap room. I was totally surprised by this request, and the way she chose to let me know, but I was able to accommodate them for that night.

However, when I got back to my room, I looked at the two Information Forms that they had filled out. In the question, *"List any serious physical disabilities or limitations",* the space was left blank. I had no warning that they needed a handicap room or that they both had walking problems.

During the night, I woke up thinking about this situation and the fact that we had five more days before the tour was over. I decided that I had to put an end to their trip before we left the next morning. In part, this was because we were heading into territory that was more remote and would be harder for them to rent a car or have someone come for them.

During the night, I hand-wrote a release form for them to sign and wrote them a check for a full refund. Although a full refund was not promised in my terms and conditions, I wanted them to have some incentive to agree to leave the tour.

The next morning after breakfast, I went to their room and told them I had made a decision that this tour was going to be too difficult for them and that I was going to give them a full refund. I was firm in my decision that they could not continue with us. I told them they needed to make their own arrangements for the trip home, by calling her husband, taking the train or renting a car.

The ladies were not happy, but I did not back down. My mind was made up and I was not giving them a choice. They reluctantly signed the release form, I gave them my check, and we parted company.

On the bus, as were pulling out of the motel parking lot, I announced that I had terminated the tour for the two ladies and had given them a full refund. There was immediate applause from the group. They had seen the behavior of the ladies and agreed that they should not continue on the tour.

Meal Selections

Some restaurants used on our tours would offer a selection of two or three entrees for a lunch or dinner. If the restaurant requested a pre-count a day or two in advance of the meal, I would include a Meal Selection form in the envelope along with the Confirmation Letter. Our travelers would then return all the paperwork along with their check in the return envelope.

In some cases, if the meal selection was for a lunch or dinner later in the tour, I would hand out the meal selection form on the bus and have them complete it and I would collect them. Then I would tabulate the results and make a call to the restaurant with the count for each selection.

See Figure 21 for an example of a Meal Selection Form.

Handling Final Payments

When the checks and forms began coming back, I first wrote the amount of payment into my handwritten reservation book on the line with the guest's name. When the due date was one or two days past, I would call the guest and inquire if the payment had been mailed. Often they had forgotten and would promise to get it in the mail that day.

On very rare occasions, when I called they told me they had decided to cancel. I would have preferred that they call me earlier with the bad news, but it's best to know sooner rather than later.

When I had a late cancellation, I was usually able to go to the next guest or guests on my waiting list and tell them I had good news for them – "I now have room for you to go". More often than not, they were very pleased with the call and were overjoyed that they could be included on the tour. In that case, I added this tour to their customer record and sent a confirmation letter out to them right away.

Badges, Luggage Tags & Boarding Passes

There are numerous things that need to be done in the week before you begin greeting your guests at the bus. I used a checklist to make sure I didn't forget anything.

See Figure 22 for a copy of my checklist.

First, using my computer and my customer records system under Lotus *Approach*, I made sure that the individual record for each of my travelers had the tour code entered into the "Tours" field for the upcoming tour. The code I used was two letters to indicate the tour (DV for Death Valley) and two numbers to indicate the year (12 for 2012).

The name(s), address, and other customer information would have been entered into the system when the traveler called for a brochure, to sign up for this tour, or it would have been in my system from their participation in an earlier tour.

To enter the tour code into all the right records, I entered each last name, one at a time, into the system and hit enter. I then entered ;DV12 into the Tours field for each tour participant. The semicolon allows the system to separate this code from the one ahead of it, if any. If DV12 is the first tour, the semicolon is not needed.

When I had entered the tour code into all the records of people who had reservations for the tour, I then printed a Bus Manifest to check against my handwritten reservation book to make sure that I had everyone on the list and that if someone had cancelled this tour the tour code had been removed.

When I had an accurate list, I could then prepare stick-on labels (1"x2 5/8", 30 labels per letter size sheet). The name tag had preferred first name (as opposed to legal first name) and last name, the luggage tags and boarding passes just showed last name.

It was very rare that I had two individuals or couples with the same last name on the same tour. If I did, I would usually just handwrite the first name or initial on the luggage tags and boarding passes rather than do a special run to add that on my computer.

See Figure 23 for examples of the Name Badge, Luggage Tag and Boarding Pass.

See Figure 24 and Figure 25 for an example of the labels used on Name Badges, Luggage Tags and Boarding Passes.

The luggage tag was a bright neon pink, very easy to see on an airport carousel or among other bags.   These labels need to be specially ordered since they are not readily available at office supply stores.

The Group Meeting Place

When establishing your business, you need to find a suitable place for your group to meet, park their car, and check in for your tour. Ideally, this should be a place that is convenient for your travelers, safe for their vehicle and close by for most of your travelers.

In large cities, where the group is flying to the destination, the airport is often the meeting place, but in small cities and towns like Lake Havasu City, we left for every one of our tours by chartered bus from our parking lot.

In my case, after meeting in a super market parking lot for our first five van tours, I realized that we needed something better. I saw a fenced lot on a major street in Lake Havasu City that was adjacent to a Best Western motel. I talked to the front desk person and was advised I would need to talk to the owner who lived in Oregon but was expected to be on the property the next week.

The next week, I met the owner and when I proposed to rent the parking lot for our tour parking and have the driver stay overnight in the motel, he was rather uninterested. When I asked why, he said he was concerned with the liability of having people meet and park in his parking lot.

When I stated that I had a $1,000,000 liability policy and I could add his motel and parking lot as an "additional insured" to take away his risk, he got interested. In 19 years we never had an accident in the parking lot or an insurance claim of any kind. Adding the parking lot to my liability insurance did not cost any additional premium.

The motel owner suggested a rate of $50 for the first day and $25 for each additional day that we would park in the lot. For a 3-day tour, that would calculate to $100 and when divided by 40 travelers, it added just $2.50 to the price of the tour.

I quickly agreed to that rate, and twenty years later, the new owners of Bartlett Tours are still paying the same rate, but to a different owner. This lot was about 25,000 square feet and was only used occasionally when a boater wanted to park his boat and trailer in the lot overnight.

Our tour parking was soon bringing the motel owner between $1,500 and $2,000 a year on a lot that had never earned any income before. It is located on a main street and has two double gates, easily accommodating our charter buses.

Since we have to charter our buses from either Phoenix or Las Vegas, the driver comes in the night before and I have reservations for him at the motel. He parks the bus in the lot, locks the gate and goes to his room.

Before we leave on tour, or often the afternoon before, we attach a 6 foot banner to the fence with the words, "Bartlett Tours". For the first-time guest, it assures them they have come to the right place for their tour. But, more importantly, this banner shows hundreds of other people in town that Bartlett Tours is traveling again.

Many of our regular travelers would tell us that after seeing the banner on the fence, and seeing all the cars parked inside, they would go home and check our brochure to see where we were touring.

If you can find any way to promote your tour business with a sign or banner at your parking area, be sure to take advantage of the opportunity. Adding your phone number to the banner would encourage new prospects to call and learn more about your tours.

You may not be as fortunate as I have been with locating a parking lot. But, I would encourage you to look in your town for a fenced lot that is not being used. If you can't find a fenced lot, look for a large lot next to a motel where semi trucks sometimes park.

Make sure your parking doesn't interfere with the truck area and ask the motel owners to have their employees keep an eye on the cars. Even though it isn't secured with a fence, if it's near a motel there will be activity and the vehicles parked there should be safe.

On the morning of our departure, we set up a small table near the bus for our guests to come to and check in. Of course, we greeted them enthusiastically and, if they were new to our tours, we would ask their name to enable us to find their badge, luggage tag and boarding pass.

If you are operating as a husband and wife team, introduce your spouse to them right away and welcome them. Hand them their professional-looking name tag right away. If this is an overnight tour, you will want to have luggage tags to hand them. Make sure they put the luggage tags on their bags before the driver loads them.

In addition to the name tags and luggage tags, we had a boarding pass for each guest or married couple. We didn't let anyone board the bus when they arrived at our parking lot. We had a second table that had two gallon jugs of coffee (regular and decaf) and three or four dozen fresh bakery cookies.

We asked our guests to enjoy the coffee and cookies and meet other people and we would call the boarding passes about 10 minutes before our scheduled departure.

The boarding pass, in our case, a pink 3x5 card, had a computer-printed label with their last name on it and a hand-printed number in the upper corner. This number was the order in which they signed up for the tour, not how early they arrived at the parking lot.

When everyone had arrived at the parking lot, about 10 minutes before departure, we began boarding by calling the numbers in order. I stood outside by the bus door and talked with each person as they entered, again making sure they understood that they could sit in any empty seat.

This system worked great over the years and virtually eliminated any friction about who got the front seat! The ones who really earned the front seat at the start of the tours were the ones that made their reservation earliest. Even they didn't get to keep the front seat since we rotated the seats each day, as explained below.

The reason I didn't add the numbers to the boarding passes when we put the name labels on is to allow for cancellations. I usually waited until the evening before our tour departure to add the numbers. Again, the boarding passes were numbered in the order of their sign-up for the tour.

The boarding pass served two purposes. First, it kept people from arriving an hour early to get the front seat on the bus. They soon found out that there was an advantage in signing up for the tour early, but not in arriving at the parking lot early. Before they boarded in sequence, they were told that they could sit in any open seat, but not our seat behind the driver.

The boarding passes served as the means to rotate the seats at the end of each day so that every person was treated equally.

Occasionally, you will get the person who tells you at the parking lot that they get car sick and will need to sit in the front seat. The answer to that is NO! I carried over 7,300 passengers and never gave into that.

First, I would tell them that ours was a very modern and comfortable bus and that I've never had anyone get sick on our tours (True!). But, if they persisted, I would tell them that I would seat them in the third row and leave them there for the duration of the trip. Often, when they saw that they couldn't bluff their way, they would agree that they probably would be OK rotating with everyone else.

Getting ready for departure on the first day required the preparation of several items, as listed below:

- Name tags with preferred first name and last name for each guest.

- Luggage tags – one for each person for their large suitcase.

- Boarding Passes – one for each couple with their last name only. Two people traveling together would get one boarding pass with two last names. A single traveler would get one boarding pass with their last name.

- Guest list – an alphabetical list showing all passengers and the number of tours for each of them (this can be impressive to first-timers). We always had this list on each seat before any guest stepped on the bus.

- Guest Itineraries – only if there are significant changes since the Confirmation Letter was sent.

- Meal selection sheet – Used when there are two or three menu choices and the restaurant needs a count before your arrival.

We always arrived at our parking lot at least fifteen minutes before we asked our guests to arrive. This gave us time to check the bus for cleanliness, talk with the driver, and discuss the tour route. The driver will normally have the luggage bays open for the checked luggage.

We made sure the driver understood that all bags had to pass by our table and had to have a bright pink Bartlett Tours tag on before they went into the luggage area.

Some people would bring a small carryon that they didn't need to take on board the bus. This was especially true if we were just doing a bus transfer to an airport or to the cruise pier in Los Angeles. We would ask them to set that near the front tire and that the driver would load those in the first luggage bay. We made it clear, however, that they would be responsible for picking up that carryon when they exited the bus at our destination.

Remember to get on the bus early and put your escort material on the front seats behind the driver. Most buses today have 56 seats. You are going to use several of the seats for your own use. This is also the time to put a copy of the Guest List on each seat. We actually put one list on each two seats, then early in the tour I would announce that I had extra guest lists and would give another where there were two unrelated people sitting together.

See Figure 26 for an example of a Guest List.

If you are leading the tour as husband and wife, you will both probably want to sit in the two front seats behind the driver. Even if you escort a tour alone, you will want these two seats and will use one of the seats for your notes and tour material. Most of today's buses have a very small desk at the front seat for you to use as escort and the microphone will be available at those seats.

If the tour is all by bus, you will probably want to take an ice chest along for bottled water. The best place for that is in the two seats in the very back next to the restroom. These are the least desirable seats for passengers, so that leaves 52 of the 56 seats for your paying passengers. In other countries the available number of seats is less because the buses generally are smaller.

If, on the other hand, you are doing a transfer to an airport, you won't want to take an ice chest because the bus will be leaving you at the airport and doing other charters. So, we handed everyone a bottle of water as they entered the bus and let them know that we weren't carrying extra water. When everyone had a bottle of water, we put the ice chest in our vehicle at the parking lot.

Management Details While On the Bus

As soon as everyone was seated on the bus, and we had put our tables and coffee gear in our car, we got on and I welcomed everyone and thanked them for being on time. Then, before we moved, I introduced our driver for the tour and made sure everyone understood that he or she was part of our "team". I then stepped off the bus to allow the driver to move out of our fenced parking lot and wait for me while I locked the gate.

Once back on board, I took the microphone and assured everyone that we were all going to have a great time on this tour. You want your guests to feel your excitement for the tour and you want to give them the feeling that you are going to make sure everyone has a good time.

I would always say, "This tour is our 165th tour", using whatever number was correct. By giving the number of the tour, it showed new guests that we had been doing this for a while and we had a track record. I always made sure to talk into the microphone with a clear voice and ask if those in the back could hear me. You or the driver can easily adjust the volume with controls on the dashboard.

At this point I used to say, "Patty and I run our tours on time, so at each stop I will give you the exact time and tell you what time you should be back in your seat ready for the wheels to roll."

Our guests received a general itinerary with their Confirmation Letter. This is so that they knew what to expect each day, what time we're leaving each morning, and times for meals, but not each stop and start. However, before we step off the bus for any stop, I announce the current time, tell them how long we will be at this stop, and give them the time to be back on the bus, seated, ready to move on.

Never say to your guests, "Be back around two o'clock". That instruction is imprecise and therefore your guests will think being 5 or 10 minutes late shouldn't be a problem. Instead, I will say, "The bus will leave at two o'clock sharp". I let them know that if they are not on the bus at the appointed time, Patty and I will go looking for them.

We don't try to embarrass anyone, but I announce on the bus that if we have to go find them, that as we are walking them back to the bus, there are at least 40 pairs of eyes watching and thinking, "Oh, I'm glad that's not me"! The announcement is done with some humor, but it really works. I've had people tell me that they've never been on a tour that ran on time and can't begin to tell me how much they appreciate this part of our tours.

Nothing is worse than having 40 or more people that came back on time, sitting on the bus waiting for a couple who thinks their schedule is more important than that of everyone else. You must make people understand that you just don't allow anyone to be habitually late. In all of the 171 tours and cruises that we conducted, lateness was rarely a problem.

I showed everyone the red "spider" that we used to indicate which side would be getting off the bus first at the next stop. I also explained at this point that we would always exit the bus with one side standing and exiting in order while the other side stayed seated. When the last person on side 1 passed the first row of those still seated, the second side could all stand and exit front to rear.

Of course, it's important that the "spider" be moved to the other side of the bus after each stop. That was Patty's responsibility and on the rare occasion that she forgot to move the spider, she got gently reminded by those sitting on the side where the spider should have been moved.

See Figure 27 for a look at our "spider".

Next, I gave a short review of the features of the bus. I explained how to tilt the seat backs, how the arm rests worked and explained that the bus had a restroom in the back, BUT that it was for emergencies only.

I explained that we had rest stops planned about every two hours and that we preferred that our guests not take a chance on moving around the bus due to the possibility of falls. I said that if the driver needs to hit the brakes or swerve to avoid an accident he will do it and won't have time to give a warning.

I always bragged to our guests about the chartered bus pointing out that "our" bus was nearly new and was a "top of the line" touring coach. I named the charter bus company and noted that they were a very reputable company with a total of 60 buses (or whatever the number was) in their fleet.

I always wanted to make our travelers aware that we were providing top-notch, quality transportation from a reliable source. By the way, we much preferred Prevost buses but sometimes have used Setra's, Van Hool's or MCI J-Models. Almost all late-model buses are 45 feet long and seat 56 passengers, but each maker has different features and most escorts have their favorites.

Getting Everyone Acquainted

On the first morning of each tour, after I had pointed out features of the bus and reviewed the itinerary for the day, I asked everyone to get acquainted with their fellow travelers. I asked them to introduce themselves to the people in front and back of them and across the aisle, and tell them where they were from or where they lived in town. As soon as I made this suggestions, the noise level in the bus went way up, which is exactly what I wanted.

After the get acquainted time, about 10-15 minutes, I told everyone that I was going to call the names from their printed list in alphabetical order and ask them to answer just two questions:

- How long have you lived in Lake Havasu City or how long have you been coming here as a winter resident?

- Where did you live prior to moving to Lake Havasu City or where do you spend your summers if you are a winter resident?

We always provided a printed list of the guests on the tour on each seat when our guests boarded the bus. I suggested they follow along on the printed list to make it easier to remember names as I interviewed each person. It was always interesting to watch what happened during the time of introductions.

I used a clipboard with the Bus Manifest on it so that I could mention a few of the other tours that each returning traveler had been on with us. This bus manifest showed the tour codes and year (DV12) for each tour, and if someone had been on 25 tours, I didn't read off all the tours, but touched on a few to highlight them.

See Figure 28 for a screenshot of the Bus Manifest.

Since our city was founded in 1964, no one over 50 years of age could have been born and raised here although we've had a number of travelers that were Lake Havasu City "pioneers" because they first arrived in the late 60's or early 70's. At that time the city had no phones, no gas station and early residents had to drive 60 miles to Kingman for groceries.

It often happened that someone would say they were from, for instance, Milwaukee, and another person on the bus would turn to look for that person and say that they were raised in Milwaukee. At the next stop, they would get together to compare notes. One time, we even had two ladies who discovered, through our introductions, that they went to high school together in the mid-west many years earlier.

After the guest introductions were completed, I would tell a little about Patty and me, how long we had been in town, where we had lived before, a little about our children and grandchildren and then I would always interview our driver.

Our guests were always interested in the driver's family, how long he'd been driving and other things he was willing to tell. Then, I would usually put on some soft music and let the guests relax until we came to our first rest stop.

The initial announcements plus the guest introductions usually took about an hour and a half. Even though they may have been repetitious for some of our frequent travelers, I often got comments about how the introductions on the bus fostered conversations at our stops or at meal functions.

Commentary While Traveling

As the escort and tour manager of our tours, I had the microphone and the responsibility to point out things along the way. I researched our route using an Auto Club book initially and later Google to find interesting facts about the towns we were passing by, the stops we were going to make and anything else of interest that we saw along the way.

I was always aware of the fact that the passengers behind us did not have the same view and, if we came to an unexpected stop on the road, due to road work or an accident, I would tell them what I could see and what was happening to cause the delay. It's important to keep the people in the back seats informed so they don't feel like they are missing anything.

I was also very aware not to have private conversations or say something to those in the first few seats that I didn't share with the entire group. If you've ever been on a bus tour and heard people talking and laughing up front, you feel you're missing out on something. If that happened, I would always use the microphone to tell what we were laughing about and keep everyone informed.

Speaking of laughing, it's good to make your travelers laugh often during the tour. If you have the ability to tell jokes (and I mean <u>tell</u> them, not read them), it can add a lot to your guests' experience. Since most travelers on your bus will be older, I never told jokes that were off-color (dirty) or were ethnic. I took a folder on every tour with pages of jokes, only to remind me of the story before I told it from memory.

I would normally tell no more than two or three jokes a day, but I would always try to find situations around me that were funny and that I could point out. I have the ability to be sarcastic without offending, and there were always certain people on the bus with me that could handle a sarcastic remark, then zing me back and laugh along with everyone else.

The travel time immediately after lunch is not a good time to give important instructions or announcements. Unless, your guests know that they only have a short travel time to the afternoon attraction, many will nod off for a little nap. During these times, I tried to stay off the microphone, or if necessary to make interesting   observations of things along the way, I would use a lower tone of voice.

Getting On and Off the Bus

Early the first day I pointed out that we used a red "spider" (actually just a red yarn pom-pom about 3" in diameter) at the front of the bus to indicate which side of the bus is to get off first at the next stop.

We attached the pom-pom to a 3/8", 1 1/2" long spacer nut, as a weight, and put that into the groove that runs at the bottom of the racks above the seats. I provide this detail because it took us a while to find something that worked.

See Figure 27 for a picture of the "spider" and the spacer nut (referred to earlier).

I explained to our travelers that at each stop, we asked everyone on the side with the red spider to stand, and all the people on the other side to stay seated until the last person from the exiting side is at the front. Then, all the people on the other side can stand and move forward to get off the bus. This is the most efficient way to leave the bus and it gives each person a chance to grab a jacket or hat from the rack above their seat without holding up the others.

I also quickly pointed out that when they returned to the bus after a stop, we would appreciate it if they would move directly to their seat and be seated as quickly as possible. If we should happen to be loading during a rain, it's imperative that everyone move quickly to get the last people in the bus and out of the rain.

Water and Snacks While Traveling

I should mention once again, that my wife, Patty, has been an integral part of our business from the start. She has helped decide on our tour schedule, accompanied me on all scouting trips and, generally been an excellent sounding board on every tour idea we've had.

On the bus, Patty serves our travelers with bottled water and a snack mid-morning and mid-afternoon when we have a full day of travel. She serves the bottles with two small plastic cups on top of the bottle and we ask seat-mates to share the water.

With 50 people on board, to give each person a bottle of water, we would have had to carry two large ice chests. By asking them to share one 16.9 ounce bottle, which has always been sufficient, we were able to put up to 28 bottles into one ice chest and serve the water cold.

I always explained this before Patty served the first time and explained that we tried a larger ice chest, but "Patty just couldn't carry one that big up the bus stairs and over her head to the back of the bus". That got a laugh as well as making a point.

The treats Patty has served over the years ranged from trail mix and breakfast bars to Snickers candy bars and everything in between. One caution however - don't serve popcorn! We served boxes of popcorn once and our driver asked us never to do that again. He said he was finding popcorn in the seats and on the floor for a week after our tour.

Everyone loved Patty's treats! Plus, they liked being served. She served them because it showed a higher level of service than if we passed a basket with treats around the bus or let them get their own water from the back. She got the chance to interact with our guests and often kid with them while she was serving. She often had the whole bus laughing at something that she said or did. Above all, it kept our travelers seated and safe.

Rotating Seats on the Bus

We chose at the very beginning of our tour business to rotate seats on the bus each day. After everyone was off the bus and in the hotel at the end of the day, I would rotate the pink boarding passes three (3) seats in a clockwise fashion.

Of course, the ones near the front on the left (driver side) would rotate around to the right (door side) and the ones on the right in the rear of the bus would rotate to the left side.

The boarding passes were left on the seats for the next morning so that each person could walk down the aisle the next morning until they found their boarding pass.

To make the boarding pass system work requires that you ask everyone to leave their boarding pass on the seat or wedged into the head rest in front of them, especially upon arrival at your hotel.

Ask them not to put the boarding pass in their purse or pocket, because if you make a count of passengers after a stop and you find you are missing someone, you can look at the boarding pass on their seat and quickly determine who is missing and who you need to look for.

I have always said that tour directors consider "Gift Shop" two four-letter words. The most common problem where there is a gift shop is that ladies will often look at things until they realize the bus is about to leave, then they get in line to buy one or two of the items. To avoid this, I would usually walk through the gift shop and say to any of our travelers, "the bus leaves in 5 minutes". That usually gets them moving.

The use of the boarding passes to rotate the seats keeps everything fair. Moving three seats at a time makes it possible for a couple starting out near the back on a five day tour to be near the front on the fifth day. In fact, first-time guests would often end up in the front seat. This showed our first-timers that we did not play favorites on our tours.

A few of my seasoned travelers figured out my rotation system and would count back a number of seats on the driver's side to allow them to end up in the front seat for a particularly scenic day of the tour. I always figured this was one way they could give themselves preferential treatment, and I was fine with it.

Arrival at your Hotel

When we arrived at our hotel or motel for the night, I asked everyone to stay on the bus while I went in to get the room keys. While I was in the lobby, I also asked where the elevator was located and where breakfast would be served (if offered) the next morning.

I also looked at the keys to see if there was a "code" that I needed to understand. The first number in the room number is usually the floor within the hotel, but sometimes our group would be in more than one building on the hotel property and the key number indicated the building as well. It helps if you can explain this before people get off the bus.

When I returned to the bus with key packets, I asked that everyone stay seated so I could move up and down the aisle with the keys. Usually the packets have the last name and room number written on the outside to make them easy to hand out. Having our guests seated made it easier to find them when I called their names. I also explained about the room numbers and where to find the elevators and the breakfast area.

At the first hotel, I also told them that if they had a problem with the TV or the toilet, to call the front desk and ask for help. If they didn't get assistance within a reasonable time, I then suggested they call me and I would get involved. I told them not to live with a problem and then tell me about it the next morning when it would be too late to get the problem fixed.

If we were having dinner in the hotel, I would give them the banquet room name and an idea how to find it from the lobby. If we were going to a restaurant for dinner, I reminded them what time we would be leaving the hotel and approximately what time we would return.

Before letting our guests off the bus, I would remind them to leave their boarding pass on the seat so that I could rotate the seats. If they wanted to leave a cap or a sweater on the seat, I would rotate that as well. But, if they left an opened bottle of water, we discarded it. After everyone was in the hotel and luggage was being delivered to their rooms, I would rotate the seats by moving the boarding passes.

If someone got off the bus and didn't leave their boarding pass, I would leave a blank 3x5 card with a "?" on it. The next morning, the offending guest would usually find their seat by remembering who was sitting in front or behind them. If they had lost their boarding pass, I would then make them a handwritten boarding pass for the rest of the tour.

Music and Videos on the Bus

All quality tour coaches have stereo sound systems with a CD player and a DVD player available for your use. It's best to familiarize yourself with the operation so that you can do it rather than distract the driver to have him do it for you.

The DVD player is generally in the luggage rack above the escort's seats. The driver needs to push a button on the radio for "video", and then you can insert the DVD and push "play". The video plays on multiple small screens throughout the bus. Volume control is on the radio in the center of the dashboard. Some of the later buses we chartered had a remote so that the tour escort could adjust volume.

Some tour leaders play games with their guests on a long day of travel. I was never comfortable doing that. To me, it seemed childish. I sometimes played an easy-listening CD after the introductions the first morning and on long stretches of travel. This was always well received by our guests.

I did not usually show videos during the day while we were traveling unless they were background information on the next attraction. Having a video with background on an historic area or national park adds to the overall experience.

However, if we were traveling after dark on our way home from a tour, I had several humorous videos that I liked to play. These videos were good, clean fun and it made our travel after dark go by much more quickly.

The videos I tended to use more than any others were comedy routines from Yakov Smirnoff, a comedic entertainer in Branson, Missouri, and Carl Hurley, a down-home comedian from Eastern Kentucky. I had about four or five different videos from each and tried not to repeat their use too often.

Other videos that our guests really liked were from Terry Fator, a very funny ventriloquist and singer in Las Vegas and Jeanne Robertson, a stand-up comedian with a slow, southern drawl. Any of these can be found online by using Google. It's good to keep your travelers laughing and videos can help, especially at night!

Frequent Traveler Awards

About the second year of Bartlett Tours, I realized we had some travelers who were coming up on their fifth tour with us. I decided I wanted to do something to recognize them for their loyalty and their continued travel with us.

I came up with the Bartlett Tours "Frequent Traveler Award" that would be given to each person or couple on their fifth tour. This was not something that they would display in their home. It was to be used for lunch of dinner at one of the finest restaurants in Lake Havasu City.

To make that work, I met with the General Manager of Shugrue's Restaurant and established an account with the restaurant. I gave him a copy of the Frequent Traveler Award printed on blue card stock so that he could show his waiters and managers. This enabled them to recognize the award recipients and congratulate the guests on their "award" when they came in to redeem it for dinner.

See Figure 43 for a sample of our Frequent Traveler Awards.

It wasn't long before we realized we had travelers that were coming up on their tenth tour, so we decided to give out the Frequent Traveler Award on each fifth tour (i.e. 5, 10.15, 20, 25, etc). In the 19 years we had Bartlett Tours, we gave out these certificates for dinner to a total of 685 travelers.

I gave out the awards on the last segment of each tour. When I announced the travelers' name and the number of tours, the others on the bus broke out in applause. I could see that the award winners were enjoying the attention.

As Shugrue's added two other restaurants to their chain, I included Barley Brothers and Javelina Cantina to the award, so that each traveler had their choice of restaurant for their dinner.

We often got phone calls or notes from people thanking us for the award and telling us how much they enjoyed having dinner "on us".

This type of recognition brings back way more than it costs. You can be sure that they have told their friends about receiving the dinner recognition as a "thank you" for their continued travel and they'll tell their friends again when they have enjoyed that wonderful dinner.

Selling Your Future Tours While on the Bus

During the last segment of each tour or transfer, I passed out copies of my current brochure listing future tours. Then, I would take the microphone and tell a little about each tour highlighting the attractions, the beauty of the area, and the fun of making new friends.

At the end of my future tours talk, I passed back small green slips that had space for the travelers name and three lines for them to sign up for future tours. I would then be available to go down the aisle to answer any question an individual traveler might have

Later, I would announce that I would be coming back to pick up any slips and deposits that were ready. If they had the slip ready but didn't have a check with them for the deposit, I just asked them to send the check when they got home.

Using this approach of selling on the bus, I would always end up with a number of future tour sign-ups; sometimes as many as fifteen or twenty. Others would ask questions and say that they were going to think about it and let me know.

There was no "high pressure" to sign up on the bus, but if your guests have had a good time on the tour, they are more likely to sign up for another tour, or two, while the excitement is still there. When they get home and go back to their everyday routine, the excitement wears off very quickly.

I would also suggest to our travelers that if they had a good time on the tour, seeing new things and meeting new people, that they invite their friends to join them on the next tour. This gets them talking about their tour and selling their friends on traveling with our tour company.

At the End of the Tour

When you get close to your parking lot after a tour, take a few moments to reflect with your guests on the elements of the tour and bring back some pleasant memories. Thank your guests for traveling with you and ask them to tell their friends about your tours.

I always encouraged them to take one or two of our brochures to give to friends. Our greatest source of new travelers was from word-of-mouth. A recommendation from a friend is the best advertising you can get, and it costs you nothing.

When you arrive in your parking lot, people are always anxious to get off the bus, gather their luggage, and drive home. Remind them that the driver will be unloading 45-50 pieces of luggage and that their luggage may not be the first off the bus. You need to tell them that lots of luggage looks alike, so make sure they look at the bright pink luggage tag to make sure they are taking their luggage home with them.

In some cases I asked them to stay on the bus another few minutes and I would help the driver line up the luggage. I also asked them to make sure they didn't walk between the bus and the luggage, because they would be in the way and might get knocked over by the driver or me while unloading the bays.

Teaming Up with your Bus Driver

The bus driver, or motorcoach operator as they are sometimes called, should become an integral and important part of each tour. They cannot be just a truck driver who now drives a bus. The driver needs to be first and foremost, a good and safe driver, but to be driving your tour, he or she needs to have a personality and know how to get along with people. He also needs to be in uniform or at least have a neat appearance while on the job.

Over our 19 years in the tour business, we had quite a number of drivers since we left Lake Havasu City by bus on every one of our 171 departures. The vast majority of these drivers were very good, but we had five or six that we liked especially well and that drove for us for several years each.

Each one of these drivers became a part of our team, and we treated them with total respect. If for some reason, we made a wrong turn, I would take responsibility for the error and if we needed to turn around in a shopping mall parking lot, I would tell our guests that we came this way because I wanted them to see this beautiful mall. Of course, they usually knew that we had made a wrong turn but they got a good laugh out of the situation.

When you are just starting out in the tour business, if a driver does a good job, give him a nice tip, thank him, and then the next day call dispatch and/or your sales person at the bus company and tell them what a good job he or she did for you. If he was really good, ask that, wherever possible, you would like him to drive for you on your future tours.

By the way, I've referred to drivers as "he" or "him". Over the years, the majority of drivers we worked with were men, but we had a number of women drivers who were equally as good.

Driving a bus requires a lot of physical effort each day loading and unloading 40 to 50 large suitcases at each hotel, often cleaning the windshield and windows several times on a tour, and checking the engine each morning, so women may not be as attracted to the job as men are.

Our "regular" drivers were not always available to do "transfers". A transfer is the travel to and from an airport or cruise terminal. For transfers, we often had drivers that were new to us, but were generally well experienced and personable.

Maintaining a good relationship with the sales person at the bus company helps to assure that you will get a driver who is satisfactory to you. If you are not satisfied with a driver, be specific when you report that back to your contact so that they know you really care about getting a good driver.

Beware of a driver who wants to carry on a conversation with the passengers in the front seats and who wants to tell jokes and otherwise entertain. If you have that experience, you must speak to the driver right away in a very quiet voice and explain to him that you do not want him to do this. The passengers in front may actually enjoy the entertainment but passengers in the back will feel like they are missing out on something.

Informing and entertaining your travelers is your job and responsibility and the driver is to drive and keep your passengers safe and secure. The time for him to talk and joke with your guests is when he is assisting them on and off the bus or during meal times when he is seated with your travelers.

Tipping the Driver on a Tour

It is normal practice on a tour to encourage your travelers to offer a gratuity to the driver. This is best done on the next-to-last stop on the tour. For instance, if you have some distance to travel on the last day to get back to your home base and need a rest stop at some point in that travel, that is the best time to have your guests tip the driver.

Like me when I started my business, you might think, "why not have them tip the driver when we get to our parking lot"? The reason is this: when you pull into your parking lot, people are anxious to get off the bus, find their luggage and get on their way home.

When passengers get off the bus, the driver may still be working to get the luggage out of the underneath bays. He doesn't have time to accept tips and properly thank the giver. In the confusion, I found that people sometimes forgot to give their tip to our driver, or chose to slip away in the confusion and give no tip at all.

Don't ever pass a hat, a bucket or a sack for the driver's tip! People will look at all the bills and think that it looks like a lot of money, so they may decide either to tip less or to skip tipping totally. This isn't fair to the driver.

What worked well for us and the driver was that at least a half-hour before the last rest stop, we passed out small envelopes to our travelers with a half-page guide showing a suggested tipping amount for this particular tour. They took an envelope, read the tipping instructions, and passed the remaining envelopes and the instructions to the travelers behind them.

The amount of the driver tip may vary by location. I would ask your sales person at the bus company what their drivers are normally receiving for overnight tours. In the later years of our tour business, we suggested an amount of $2.00 to $3.00 per person, per day. We then did the calculation for them on the handout sheet. If it was a 3-day tour, our handout showed that the range of suggested gratuity was from $6.00 to $9.00 per person.

See Figure 29 for our handout on Driver Tipping.

116

I announced that they could put their gratuity in the envelope and perhaps write a short thank you note to our driver on the outside of the envelope. Then, when they got off the bus, they could hand it to the driver, shake his hand or give him a hug if they wanted to, and properly thank him for his service.

At this last rest stop before tours' end, I always asked the driver to step back and let me help them off the bus. This gave each person a little more time with the driver and didn't slow down the others getting off the bus. I also found that most of our travelers wrote a little note on the envelope which I found the drivers really enjoyed reading later.

Because we often gave recognition to our driver, thanking him for a long day of travel or driving through difficult terrain, I believe our guests always gave the higher suggested amount of gratuity and our drivers always felt well compensated. This makes for a loyal driver who will go out of his way to satisfy not only the tour escort, but each and every one of his passengers.

In addition to the guest gratuity, I always gave the driver a gratuity of $50 or $60 from Patty and me. This was to demonstrate to the driver that he (or she) was a key part of the success of our tour and that we appreciated him and considered him a member of our "team".

Tipping the Driver on a Transfer

As explained earlier, a transfer is that part of a tour or cruise that takes you from your home starting point to an airport or cruise terminal to begin your excursion.

For instance, since Lake Havasu City is 150 miles from the Las Vegas airport, 200 miles from the Phoenix airport, and 330 miles from the Los Angeles cruise terminal and the Los Angeles International Airport, if we were going on a cruise or flying somewhere to begin our tour, the first and last part of the trip was a transfer.

117

On a transfer, we included the gratuity in the cost of the tour or cruise and did not ask our guests to tip the driver individually. Instead, when we arrived at our transfer destination, after the guests were on their way to check-in, I tipped the driver directly. The tip I gave was generally $50.

If the transfer involved an overnight before our check-in, as it would if we had an early morning flight, and the driver stayed overnight with us, I tipped him $75 or $100. Of course, the drivers' room was paid by us and was included in the costing of the tour or cruise. If we had a dinner and breakfast for our group, the driver was always included.

Expanding the Distance and Length of your Tours

After your first few tours, you will begin to understand what makes a good tour and what your travelers like and want. Hopefully, your satisfied customers will begin to spread the word about your tours and your clientele will begin to expand. Your early guests will sometimes suggest future tours that they would like to go on. Don't hesitate to ask what other types of tours your travelers would like to see.

Your best advertising will always be "word of mouth" recommendations by travelers who return happy and want to make sure that your business (and their opportunity to travel) is successful and continues in a profitable manner. At the end of each tour, ask your satisfied clients to tell their friends about your tours and encourage them to call for a tour brochure.

As your repeat business expands, your travelers will expect you to offer new and exciting destinations for them. If your primary market is full-time residents of your area, they will lose interest if you repeat the same tours year after year. So, the process of scouting new tours will be a continuing effort.

You need to decide the area in which you are comfortable conducting tours on your own. For my tour business, we decided that we could conduct tours within the Western states of Arizona, California, Nevada, New Mexico, Southern Utah and Southern Colorado. These states were close enough that we could quite easily scout a tour and be reasonably knowledgeable about their features.

The tours that we offered in these areas were as follows:

❖ Sedona and the Verde Canyon Train
❖ Broadway musicals at the Gammage Auditorium, Arizona State University
❖ San Diego Christmas Lighted Boat Parade
❖ Rose Parade in Pasadena

- ❖ California Coast and the Hearst Castle
- ❖ Canyon de Chelly and Monument Valley (northeast Arizona)
- ❖ Hollywood and Universal Studios
- ❖ Palm Springs Follies
- ❖ San Francisco and the Napa Wine Country
- ❖ Death Valley and Scotty's Castle
- ❖ Lawrence Welk Resort Musical Shows (Escondido, California)
- ❖ Tucson and Southern Arizona
- ❖ Southern California Cultural Tour (The Getty Museum and the Pantages)
- ❖ Lord of the Dance (Las Vegas)
- ❖ Arizona Fall Color (White Mountains area in Eastern Arizona)
- ❖ The Gold Country of California
- ❖ Utah Canyon Country (Southern Utah)
- ❖ Christmas Musical Shows in Southern California
- ❖ Historic Hotels of Southern California
- ❖ Durango and Mesa Verde National Park (Southern Colorado)
- ❖ Tuacahn (Broadway musicals in an outdoor amphitheater, St George, Utah)
- ❖ The Reagan Library near Simi Valley, Southern California
- ❖ Albuquerque Balloon Festival
- ❖ Lake Mead and Valley of Fire (near Las Vegas)
- ❖ San Diego Sampler Tour
- ❖ Thanksgiving on the Queen Mary (Long Beach, California)
- ❖ Wonder Valley Ranch Resort (near Fresno, California)
- ❖ Yosemite National Park in central California
- ❖ Two Rims and a Rainbow (Grand Canyon south & north rims, plus Lake Powell and the Rainbow Bridge)

Many of these tours were repeatable, but generally we would wait about three years before offering the same tour again. However, the Palm Springs Follies, Christmas Shows Tour and the Tuacahn musicals were the types that could be offered each year because they would be offering a different performance each time.

Make sure you don't book your tour calendar so full that you don't have the time to go traveling on your own to find new tours. Don't consider it a vacation when you are on a scouting trip. You will have a good time, but you want to come back with solid information and ideas that you can turn into a profitable tour.

Contracting with a Large Tour Company

Your second or third year is the time to look at going well beyond your original offering of tours. This may be the time to partner with a larger tour company and take your groups on tours that would be difficult if not impossible for you to do on your own.

In this book, I will refer to these as "major" tours.

If you have developed a record of averaging 40 or more travelers per tour in your first few years, your participants are probably ready to go further and spend more. You can partner with large nation-wide or world-wide tour companies to bring any number of travelers on their tours up to what they refer to as "full bus".

Subscribe to tour brochures from several major tour companies such as Collette, Globus, Trafalgar, and others. Cosmos is more of a budget version and a sister company of Globus. Cosmos will offer a less expensive price but at the cost of lesser accommodations and fewer meals. Of course, you can get plenty of information on these companies and their tour offerings from the Internet.

Instead of offering our own tour to a destination that was well out of our familiar territory (the Western states), we chose to contract with a large tour company that had this tour in their regular catalog of tours, had the experienced guides, had existing relationships with hotels, restaurants and attractions, and knew the important stops along the way. This arrangement with large tour companies worked very well for us and our travelers over the years.

For example, if your location and knowledge is primarily in a western state, a tour to see the New England fall colors would be difficult for you to offer unless you took the time and spent the money to go to New England to scout out a tour. I've covered scouting a tour earlier in this book, but scouting one hundreds or thousands of miles from your home area can be very expensive.

To scout a 7-day tour will usually take at least 7 to 10 days, and that is if you did a considerable amount of work on the Internet to plan your scouting trip. For instance, a hotel that sounds great may not satisfy your needs when you actually visit it and thus you may have to spend extra time finding a more suitable place to stay on the tour.

When you work with a larger tour company to do a tour out of your area or out of the country, they will determine the price and the terms of their tour. Your share of the revenue will usually be in the form of a commission which is figured as a percentage of the tour's retail price.

If you are having the larger tour company arrange for air travel, they may pay a lesser percentage or zero commission on the air portion. If you are operating your tours from a location some distance from an airport, you will need to arrange additional transportation.

This additional transportation will probably involve travel by bus to an airport to fly to the starting point of their tour. In addition, you might need to include an overnight at a hotel near the airport, dinner for the group, breakfast and a transfer to the airport the next day.

The same type of arrangements may well be necessary for the return trip. This gives you two distinct and different opportunities for profit. In addition to the commission you will receive from the larger tour company, you should plan your part of the transportation, to and from their starting point, to include a reasonable and fair profit.

Some tour companies will offer no commission but rather one "comp" (complimentary fare) for every 15 or 20 paid passengers. This indicates that they are probably targeting their business to pre-formed groups like church members, fraternal organizations or clubs where an "organizer" is putting the group together and for their effort, the organizer will get to go free, or at a reduced rate.

This "comp" arrangement usually provides a much lower return for a "for-profit" tour business, such as mine was. In this case, I would try to negotiate for a reasonable commission or a "net-net" rate. If the tour company is only willing to offer you a "comp" for you to bring them a group, I would suggest you would be much better off looking for a different company to deal with.

As an example of contracting with a large tour company for a "major" tour, I offered a tour in October, 2010 called "Back Roads of New England". It was really a New England fall color tour, but since you can't predict the weather or the turning of the leaves, I felt more comfortable downplaying the fall color theme. It did not hurt sales of the tour!

I contracted with Collette Vacations to operate the tour from Boston (their starting point) and ending in Boston, with air arrangements from Las Vegas, our closest airport, 150 miles from our base in Lake Havasu City. It was my responsibility to make the travel arrangements between Lake Havasu City, and the Las Vegas airport and return.

I made the arrangements with Collette for a "full bus" tour and the air arrangements about eighteen months in advance. In contracting for a "full bus", they agree that they will not sell this tour on this date to individuals or to other groups during the period of time that I have to sell it. That protected "sell time" is usually up until 60 days or 90 days prior to the tour start date.

For tours in the United States, a "full bus" for contract purposes usually must be a minimum of 38-44 passengers. If your sales are better than the contracted for number, you can almost always add more passengers up to about 50. This number includes you and your spouse if you are escorting the tour.

Be aware, if you don't fill the number of seats for a "full bus", you can still take your group but the tour company has the right to fill the remaining seats. Of course, the profit should still be a reasonable profit at the lower number of participants or you should consider cancelling the tour.

As a side note, in 2006, we offered a 17-day tour of China with a 4-day Yangtze River cruise. We needed 36 people for "full bus" and we ended up with only 19 including my wife and me. Taking seventeen paying passengers was still above the break-even point, and I very much wanted to see China, so we went forward with the tour.

The tour company added 15 other people, all independent travelers, to our group. It turned out that we melded together very nicely and we became one cohesive group. In fact, because I was friendly and introduced myself to the ones who were not in my group, most of them eventually looked to me for advice and suggestions.

After the date for the New England tour was confirmed and the contract accepted, I then began working to arrange the bus charter, hotels and meals that would be needed to make the tour from our home town. Even though I didn't have the flight times, experience told me that we would have an early morning flight going from west to east and losing two hours in the process.

Arizona is in the Mountain Time Zone but does not observe Daylight Savings Time, thus we are the same as California from early March to early November and the same as Colorado from early November to Early March. In planning this tour, I knew we would need to stay overnight in Las Vegas before we flew to Boston.

As I got quotes from my regular Las Vegas charter bus company and a casino hotel on the outskirts of Las Vegas, I began to compile a computer spreadsheet (*Excel*) with the quoted prices. I took a calculated risk in not adding in a second night in a hotel for our return because there was about a 50/50 chance that we would have an east to west flight that would get us in early enough that we could make it back to Lake Havasu City at a reasonable evening hour.

124

I considered our return time "reasonable" if we were able to get our guests back into our town before 9:00pm. Most would have less than a ten-minute drive from our parking lot to their home. If the flight time did not allow for a reasonable return, I would then make meal and hotel arrangements for the group and we would return home the next day.

As I determined more costs for such things as meals, skycap tips, arrival dinner in our Boston hotel the night before our tour began, etc., I added these expenses and the net per person price of the Collette tour and airfare to my spreadsheet to come up with a price for the complete tour.

I felt that this tour to New England would sell out (48-50 passengers), but for calculating a reasonable profit, I usually used a number of 40 paying passengers. If more seats are sold, the profit will be better than projected.

With this spreadsheet method, I determined I could offer the tour for $2,495 per person, double occupancy (two to a room). If a hotel night was required on our return, once I had the airline schedule, I could add that slight additional cost later with a notice enclosed with the final invoice.

As it turned out, when I received our final flight arrangements a couple of months in advance of the tour, our return flight was to arrive in Las Vegas at about 9:00pm, so an overnight was a must.

I was able to make arrangements for additional bus service from the airport to the hotel, rooms for all, and breakfast, all for just $30 additional per person, which I explained in an information sheet and added to the final invoice. Hotel rooms in or near Las Vegas are inexpensive during the week but go up considerably on the weekends.

Larger tour companies will usually provide a complimentary or "comp" tour on a ratio of one comp per 15-20 paid travelers in addition to the commission on the paid passengers. However, in dealing with Collette Vacations over the years, they were willing to offer me a "net/net" price on their tours rather than any commission or any "comp" tours.

I prefer the net/net method, without comps, since it actually makes it easier to price a tour. That way, the Collette part of the tour was just another per-person cost and I could easily include all the net costs and then price the whole tour to provide the profit that I wanted.

In using net/net pricing, it is very important to remember to include the cost of the Collette tour and airfare for you, the escorts. Policies change, and today you may not be able to get net/net pricing from Collette or other tour companies.

For the New England tour, a "major" tour conducted by Collette Vacations, see the following Figures in the Illustrations Section.

"Major" Tour Profit Projection	Figure 30
Customer Invoice	Figure 31
Important Information	Figure 32
Domestic Air Instructions	Figure 33
Driver Itinerary for Transfer	Figure 34
Sample Flyer for a "major" tour	Figure 35

During the days and weeks I was gathering the pricing data for each individual expense making up this 10-day tour, I was also gathering the same kind of data for each of the 5 or 6 other tours and cruises that I was planning on advertising in my next brochure. My October brochure usually had 12 to 15 tours described that were offered over a period of about eighteen months.

This effort of deciding on future tours, researching and gathering cost data each year took up the better part of two months. I did this during the summer, which was always our slower period due to the fact that our winter residents (often called "Snowbirds") had "flown" before our Arizona heat arrived.

Using a City Sightseeing Company

In some cases, it may be possible and cost advantageous to contract with a company that conducts day tours in your destination city. If, for instance, you are planning a tour to Washington, DC; New York City; San Antonio; or San Francisco, where you will by flying to and from the city, you will find companies that offer half and full-day tours of the city and surrounding attractions.

The largest of these sightseeing companies is Gray Line. You can find their various destinations by going online to www.grayline.com and choosing the city that you are considering. Of course, each city has other independent sightseeing companies that you can consider as well.

In past years, we have used Gray Line in San Francisco, San Antonio and Washington, DC and have been happy with their service.

The advantage is that you are hiring a bus and driver/narrator that is totally familiar with the city and probably does each tour several times each week. They know the city like no out-of-town driver could possibly know it. In addition, Gray Line has access to historic churches, national monuments, museums, etc. that would take you countless hours to arrange and schedule.

Gray Line also has numerous tours to the attractions that can be visited in a day from the origin city. For instance, in using Gray Line in San Antonio, we included a day trip to the Texas Hill Country, historic Fredericksburg, and the Lyndon Baines Johnson Ranch.

On our tour to Washington, DC we were able to add a day trip to colonial Williamsburg. In San Francisco, we added a day trip to the Napa Wine Country with two stops for wine tasting and tours at wineries.

Another advantage of using a sightseeing company is that you are not paying to have both a driver and a step-on guide – the driver/narrator acts in both capacities. Our experience has been that these driver/narrators are very good and offer a lot of interesting information about their city.

A disadvantage of using a city sightseeing company is that when your day tour is over, the bus will drop you at your hotel and you will be "bus-less" until the next morning. So, if you need a bus to take you from your hotel to a restaurant for dinner and back, you will have to pay extra and the company will probably send another bus and another driver, since your driver/narrator may have already worked a full day.

Using a sightseeing company in San Antonio worked very well for us since we had arranged for one dinner in the hotel and our other three dinners at restaurants within a three-block walk along the beautiful San Antonio River Walk. To make this work, we selected a Marriott Hotel right on the River Walk and paid a premium price for the hotel.

Even though we made it clear in our pre-tour information that participants in this tour would need to be able to walk 3-4 blocks, we had a few that decided that they couldn't make it that far. So, I got a cab for them at the hotel and the three of them shared the cost of the cab ride.

With a senior adult group, even though you make it clear that there will be walking, one or more in the group will usually have a problem and you just have to grin and bear it. Sometimes the hotel will take a few guests in one of their vans.

In conclusion, if your tour is primarily based around one city, and you are flying to that city, a sightseeing company is something to compare in cost with chartering a bus at that destination and hiring a local step-on guide. However, if your tour involves travel to several locations or states over a period of several days, (for instance a New England Fall Color Tour), a sightseeing company is not likely to be able to satisfy your needs.

Escorting Groups through Airports

When your tour or cruise requires flying to the starting point, your escorting job takes on new dimensions. There is always some nervousness when people approach an airport. Finding the right terminal, finding a place to park to unload the luggage, getting a Sky Cap to take the luggage for you, getting to the check-in counter, getting through TSA security, and finally, getting to the departure gate.

You have all these concerns when you are escorting a group to and through an airport. However, it's important that you appear calm and in complete control.

First, when the bus is stopped at an unloading curb, ask everyone to stay seated while you go to the outside check-in and talk with a Sky Cap. Tell the Sky Cap that you have a group and that you have X number of bags that you want he and a partner to move from the bus to the inside check-in. Tell them that you will be tipping them. They are usually very glad to handle a group and will grab a couple of large carts and head for your bus.

I ask the Sky Caps if the airline check-in agents will want us to go into a special group line or get in line with everyone else. Different airlines and different airports handle this differently. In addition, many airlines have kiosks for self check-in now which can be another hurdle. On occasion, if the weather is good and the Sky Caps are not busy, they will offer to handle check-in outside, avoiding lines inside.

Make sure you tell the Sky Caps to only load the large bags coming off the bus with the bright pink tags on them. The smaller carryon's will be taken from the bus by your guests and will be their responsibility to take with them on the plane.

Next, get back on the bus and tell your passengers that everything is being taken care of and to sit in place until all the bags are loaded. They will be anxious to go, but remind them that they can't check in inside until their bags are at the check-in counter.

An important note worth repeating here: the only bags that should have a bright pink tag on them are their large bags that they intend to check in, NOT any carryon's.

If, at check-in at your hometown, you have two luggage tags available for each couple, but a couple has packed in one suitcase, they may try to take the second tag for a carryon. Don't give them the extra tag!!

If one of your guests puts a bright pink tag on their carryon, the Sky Caps will likely load it with the other luggage while the passenger is still sitting on the bus. This can result in the guest being panicked because it's not at the bus when they get off. I have had this exact experience!

When the Sky Caps have all the luggage loaded and they start toward the check-in gate, I ask everybody to get off the bus, front to back, one side at a time, and follow the Sky Caps into the terminal. Before I leave the bus I thank the driver and give him his tip, usually $50. Meanwhile, Patty stays on the bus checking for anything left behind by any of our travelers. She has found passports, cameras, hats, coats, etc. so it's an important function.

Airport Check-In

Once we arrive at the inside check-in area, I ask the Sky Caps to unload the luggage beside the front of the line barriers and I tip them about $1.25 - $1.50 per bag. Remember, this has been included in the pricing of the tour, so it's not coming out of your pocket. Don't be stingy.

Sometimes, depending on how busy the airport is at that time, you can ask one of the Sky Caps to stay and help move the bags for you. This is going to earn an additional tip if they are able to help. If they are too busy with travelers outside, and you are not able to lift heavy bags, you may be able to get a couple of the more able bodied men in your group to help you.

I stand at the front of the line near the luggage and look at our name tags on the travelers coming up to the front. I then find their luggage using the bright pink tags with their names clearly shown. I, or the Sky Cap with my direction, move their bags to the front of the line so that they can have them to move to the next available agent when called.

Often the supervisor will assign three or four windows to checking in a large group. When this happens, I stay near the front and direct the next guest to the available counter. Sometimes people will get into a conversation and forget to watch for the next available agent. When I do this, I often get a "thank you" from the agents for keeping our group moving.

We tell our travelers that as soon as they have checked in, have their boarding pass, and know the departure gate, they should head for that gate. We suggest they go through security before stopping to shop or eat in case there is a delay. There may be time for them to stop and have something to eat, but emphasize that you want them in the boarding area 30 minutes before the time of departure.

Patty and I are always the last to check-in and get our boarding pass. This way we are there to help anyone who may have a problem. It also assures them that we are not leaving them on their own.

Along with their final invoice and the Important Information sheet sent well before the departure date, we include a detailed sheet explaining the "rules" that they need to know to get through security without a problem.

See Figure 33 (referenced earlier) for the "Helpful Tips for Domestic Airline Travel" sheet.

Using Kiosks to Check In

Today, more and more airlines are using Kiosks for self check-in. This can be a problem for some if they are not computer savvy. I ask at the counter if we can have an airline person in the Kiosk area to help people in our group. The airlines will generally be happy to provide assistance so your group doesn't delay the check-in process for others.

To use a Kiosk, you first must swipe a driver's license or a credit card to give the system your name. It will not charge anything to a credit card. From that information, the Kiosk will display the reservation information and walk each person through the check-in process.

If the reservations are for a couple, check-in is first one person then the other. When check-in is complete, the Kiosk will print boarding passes and deliver them at the bottom of the Kiosk.

Remind people that they are there to get a boarding pass and not to walk away from the machine without it. This is a common problem!

The last step in the self check-in process is to take your luggage to an agent at the counter who will tag it for you and send it on its way. Usually the agent doing the luggage tagging will call out the last name of the traveler when he or she has printed the tags.

With boarding pass in hand, your traveler can then make their way through the security check point and on to the departure gate. Again, ask them to be at the departure gate 30 minutes ahead of the flight time. Most airlines will start boarding 15-20 minutes ahead of scheduled departure.

Offering Ocean Cruises

Another way to expand your tour business is to offer cruises. Cruises are a very popular way to travel and they can be very profitable for the small tour operator. However, unlike contracting with a tour company for a land tour, dealing with cruise lines is often much more difficult.

You can search for cruises online or order brochures from major cruise lines such as Princess, Norwegian Cruise Line (NCL), Holland America, Royal Caribbean, Celebrity and Carnival to get an idea of what cruises are available.

Dealing with Cruise Lines

The majority of ocean cruise lines will only deal with groups through a licensed travel agency. The only way for you to deal directly with the cruise lines is for you to become an agent for a licensed travel agency. There are at least two ways to become an agent:

1. Work with an established local or regional travel agency. Many travel agencies allow you to be home based, working online with their resources and computerized systems. The advantage is that you can be a direct employee with the support, resources and benefits the agency offers.

2. Find an online host agency to start your own independent travel agency. A host agency offers travel agents services, marketing support, back office support and access to reservation portals and travel suppliers. If you work with a host agency, you work entirely on commission and usually must pay a monthly fee for their hosting services.

If you're serious about being a tour operator, be careful that you don't get sidetracked into becoming a travel agent. In my opinion, a travel agent today spends a great deal of time researching a trip for a client for very little commission.

Most people prefer to go online and make their own arrangements. The business of being a tour operator offers you a much better chance of earning good money.

I suggest you use your travel agent status only to deal with cruise lines for your group business. Dealing with individuals and their travel needs can become very time consuming and, in my estimation, much less lucrative than the group travel business. If you intend to operate your tour business without employees, and conduct eight or ten tours and cruises each year, you can be assured you won't have time to be a travel agent as well.

To work with an established travel agency, look in your local phone book under "travel". You will want to find an agency that does not conduct any of their own group tours. If you approach an agency that does tours, they will likely see you as competition and either try to discourage you or try to hire you to do tours for them.

Because of the cutting of commissions by airlines in the last decade or more, there are significantly fewer "brick and mortar" travel agencies and more agencies working out of their homes. Agencies make their money from commissions paid by airlines, cruise lines, hotels and attractions that offer a percentage commission for the agency handling the booking and dealing directly with the client.

Because these commissions have come down in the past few years, most agencies also now charge a per person fee (currently about $25) for booking individual travel in order to make up for the lower commissions being paid.

When approaching an agency about being an agent to book your cruises only, you need to make it clear that you don't intend to compete with them, but rather, you can add group business to their agency with a portion of the commissions going to them. Make sure they understand that you won't need office space or a computer and you won't be using their phone.

You will be an "outside agent". It will be up to the agency to decide how much of their commission they are willing to share with you. In my opinion, your share of the commission on the business you bring to them should be at least 50 percent and as much as 75 percent.

In my case, I was approached in 1992 by long-time IBM friends of mine who were opening a cruise-only agency near Phoenix. They asked if I was interested in becoming an outside agent for them. Before their phone call, they had no idea that I was in the process of starting a tour business.

I remember saying to them "Sure! I have no idea how to be an agent, but why not? It might fit well into my tour operation." Well, it did indeed! I was an outside agent for Sunsational Cruises for nineteen years and booked a total of 27 group cruises through their agency with a total passenger count of 1,347 or an average of 49.9 passengers per cruise.

This passenger count per cruise is slightly inflated by the fact that in 1997 and in 1999, we actually had 87 and 83 travelers respectively on two Mexican Riviera cruises requiring two buses each for our trip of 330 miles to the pier in Los Angeles. My sales added profit to their agency and, after the first group cruise I booked, I required very little support – a phone call or email every few months.

As a cruise agent, I was able to deal directly with the cruise lines, from the initial booking of the group right through to the completion of the cruise. When I talked with a cruise line, I was "Gordon Bartlett with Sunsational Cruises" booking a cruise for the Bartlett Tours group.

When booking a group cruise, there is usually a small deposit of perhaps, $25 per berth ($50 per cabin) due soon after booking. The timing of this deposit is different for different cruise lines but may be as close as 48 hours from the original booking. This deposit is something that will come out of your pocket and will be returned to you with an invoice credit at final payment time.

Most cruise lines will accept payment from your business credit card for deposits and for bookings into your group, but final payment can generally only be done with your payment to the agency and then their payment, usually online with an electronic funds transfer (EFT), to the cruise line.

When I first began booking cruises in 1995, everything was done over the phone talking to a reservation agent at the cruise line. This included the original booking of the cruise to the booking of each individual cabin as reservations came in. As you can imagine, that has changed over time with almost everything now being done online through your computer.

I missed talking with an agent but there are advantages to booking on your computer. For instance, if you want to make a booking just before you go to bed, the online booking system is ready and waiting for you. If you want to check to see if pricing has gone down on a particular category of cabin, you can check it at any time. You can still talk to a reservation agent during business hours if you have a problem or question, but you generally won't need to.

When you've gotten some experience with doing bus tours, it may be time to think about your first cruise. If you have hooked up with a travel agency, they probably have cruise brochures available in their office. Take some home and look at the variety of cruises available.

I would suggest, if at all possible, that you choose a cruise that leaves and returns from a port close enough to you that you can bus there in one day. Cruises allow boarding for several hours in the afternoon, so if the port is close enough (about 350 miles or less) you should be able to bus to the port with lunch on the way and be at the port in time for a leisurely boarding.

If it's further than a day's bus ride to the port, you may have to overnight and then have a city tour or some attraction to visit the next morning before the afternoon boarding.

Having to fly to the port adds complexity for you in having to deal with airports, security, plus luggage at both ends of the flight, and possible multiple flights for your group. But, of course, you may not have a choice and you will just have to "deal with it" and consider it a learning experience.

Once you have decided on a cruise, ask your agency for help in making the booking. Each cruise line has a different online system and they change and update them on a regular basis, so it wouldn't be helpful for me to try to give instructions in this book.

Getting your Group to the Pier

If you are in a remote location and will have to transport your group to the pier or to an airport, GREAT! This means you will be able to offer a service to your travelers that they couldn't get if they were booking a cruise as individuals. It also means some people will go with you because you are providing the transportation and allowing them to avoid driving into a congested airport or cruise terminal.

That travel before and after the cruise, is known as a profit opportunity. Don't make the mistake of showing the price of the cruise and a separate price for the travel to the port. You will want to come up with a package price that includes everything with the exception of shore excursions, which will be an individual choice, and on-board gratuities.

Why a package price? You are a tour operator, not a travel agent. You are not just selling them a cruise; you are selling them a total package. You are under no obligation to show your customers the price of the cruise because you are offering a complete package including transportation from your home town to the ship and return, possibly lunch each way, possibly an overnight and dinner, plus luggage handling at the pier.

See Figure 36 for an example of a flyer sent to those interested in a cruise.

If you have someone call and say that they have booked the same cruise that you are taking your group on and would like to go with you on your bus, say "NO".

You are not Greyhound Lines offering bus rides for a fare; you are only offering packaged travel – all or nothing. If you give in, they may tell your regular travelers that they saved money on the cost of the cruise and got all the benefits of traveling with you and your group. That will only cause problems for you!

See Figure 37 and Figure 38 for an example of a Profit Projection spreadsheet of an ocean cruise, not involving air flights.

I always did the "transfer" portion (getting to and from the ship) and the "cruise" portion of the package as separate *Excel* spreadsheets merely to simplify things.

By offering a package price, once the traveler arrives at your parking lot, the cruise package takes care of most everything else. By including all services in one package price, it's almost impossible for any of your travelers to question your price.

You will be offering a cruise that they can price and book online if they want, but in most cases the fact that you are going to be with them and take care of the transportation, parking and luggage handling, will make the difference.

Even if the man in the couple says he can do it cheaper by driving and taking care of luggage himself, his wife will usually talk him out of that because of the service you are going to provide and the enjoyment of traveling with a group.

At check-in at your hometown starting location, you will need to have cruise line luggage tags available to attach to each piece of "checked" luggage. The cruise line uses their luggage tag for sorting of the luggage once you have handed it over at the pier.

Of course, the tag will have your traveler's name and cabin number on it, but in addition it will have an indication of where the cabin is located on the ship, such as "Forward", "Mid", or "Aft" and "P" for Port side or "S" for Starboard. This aids the stewards in getting the luggage to the cabins quickly.

In the past, ship luggage tags were sent out by each cruise line pre-printed on vinyl stock. Some cruise lines may still send tags, but many have eliminated sending the tags and instead, require you, the agent, to print them on your computer printer. This, of course, shifted the burden from the cruise line to you.

The cruise line luggage tags print out on a regular 8 ½ x 11 sheet and then you have to make two folds. The resulting tag is surprisingly sturdy after it is attached with staples or strong tape. These need to be attached before you leave your home parking lot because porters will be waiting to take your luggage upon arrival at the cruise terminal.

In addition to luggage tags, I always had an envelope for each person, or one per married couple, with their bar-coded boarding pass for the ship (which you have also printed for them on your computer) and a short list of the most popular shore excursions.

Also in the envelope was a single sheet explaining the disembarkation procedure (when you get on the ship, you are "embarking"; getting off the ship at the end of the cruise, you are "disembarking"), and an invitation to an exclusive "Bartlett Tours" cocktail party on the last afternoon before the end of the cruise. I'll tell more about the party later.

Arriving at the Pier

Before you arrive at the pier, you should tell them something about the ship. You can usually tell them how to find their deck by the first digit of their cabin number. With a little detective work before the cruise, you can tell them that odd-numbered cabins are on the port (left) side, facing forward; and the even-numbered cabins are on the starboard (right) side of the ship.

Be sure to tell them what time dinner is to be served and the name of the dining room that your group will be dining in. Usually, their dining table number is shown on their room key/boarding pass which they will receive at check-in pier side.

Senior adults seem to like to be early for everything on a tour or cruise. However, most ships do not open the dining room until the exact time for dinner. The lounge near the dining room entrance will be crowded, as well as the stairwells, just before the dinner hour. It's actually better to arrive about 5 minutes after dinner time because then you can usually walk right in. Remember, everyone has a reserved seat for dinner.

Tell your guests that on the first evening, waiters will be standing by to ask their table number, or look at their cabin key card for the number, and will lead them to their table. I like to have our guests sit at tables of six and eight as much as possible, and I make those arrangements weeks in advance with the cruise line. Most people enjoy the conversation at a large table rather than being seated alone or with only one other couple.

Remember, the objective of you giving helpful information in advance is to take away any worries that they won't be able to maneuver through check-in and find their cabin on that huge ship. This "expert advice" that you offer is why people will feel comfortable traveling with you and why they will come back.

When you and your guests are ready to leave the bus, remind them that they will need three things to check in: 1) their passport; 2) their boarding pass, and 3) the credit card they intend to have all onboard expenses charged to. Remind them to take everything with them off the bus and to grab their carryon if they left it to be put under the bus.

You should make your guests aware that they will have to go through a security check and x-ray machines inside the pier building. These checks are not as rigid as airport checks and do not require you to remove your shoes. They will also be required to show their boarding pass/room key two or three times while boarding.

You might also tell them that they will be stopped along the way to the ship by photographers wanting to take their picture. Tell them they are under no obligation to purchase the pictures later and it's easier to pose than it is to try to bypass the photo stop. They will enjoy looking for their picture in the photo gallery later.

When you have briefed them during your travel to the pier, they exit the bus with confidence. You then send them on to pier check-in with only their personal carryon while you stay behind and watch the porters load the luggage on carts and move it into the warehouse for sorting before it goes on the ship.

Of course, you want to tip the porters at least $1.00 to $1.50 per bag before you leave. If there are several porters working on your 40-50 bags, give the tip to the one that came up first and he will split it among the team.

Remember, this monetary tip and one for the driver (about the same amount) must be included in what you have charged in your package price. You are not tipping them personally. You are giving them the tips you have added into your costs to come up with your selling price.

When the luggage has departed your bus, and after you have tipped the driver, get his cell phone number so that you can call him for his location at the pier when you return at the end of your cruise.

I always asked the driver to "spot" the bus at 9:00am, knowing that we would not likely get to the bus before 9:30 or 10:00. It's very disconcerting, and can cause you some nervousness, to have your group get through Immigration and Customs and then find that your bus is not there.

Make sure that you or your partner/spouse checks the bus thoroughly before you allow it to leave. Patty has found cameras, passports, coats, etc. left on the bus and your forgetful traveler will be very pleased when you bring it to them. In their haste, some will even forget their carryon's. After all is taken care of, you can then get in line for security and check-in.

You will only be minutes behind the rest of your group, so keep an eye out for anyone who may be having a problem at check-in. Just the fact that you go to them to see if there is a problem is reassuring to them that you are there to help.

Your Work, Once On-Board the Ship

Once your group is checked in and on-board, and you have found your cabin, it's time to find the dining room and check with the Maitre d' or his assistant to make sure that the seating for dinner is as you requested. It's also important for him to show you exactly which tables he has assigned to your group.

Even if the ship has free-style dining, as is the case with Norwegian Cruise Lines, rather than fixed dining, I like to make arrangements with the Maitre d' for seating as a group on the arrival evening and every second evening during the cruise.

I find that a group such as ours, traveling from our home to the pier together, is very much interested in being seated together so that they can exchange stories about their day on shore.

On the days when you don't have group reservations, guests can call ahead from their cabin to make reservations in the main dining room or in one of several specialty restaurants on board. NCL, for example, may have 10 or 12 specialty restaurants including a no-charge "fifties style" hamburger joint.

Specialty restaurants offer a higher level of service and probably a better cut of steak, but for that extra, you pay a cover charge which is currently about $20 per person. This charge, of course, is just added to your on-board account when you produce your room key.

Some people may prefer on some evenings to go to the buffet where they have endless choices and a more casual atmosphere. I've never understood exactly why people would want to do that when they have paid for a waiter in a tuxedo to serve them, but I guess some are uncomfortable with that kind of luxury.

I mentioned a cocktail party earlier. If you have more than a certain number of guests in your group, usually about 40-50, you can choose a no-cost cocktail party as one of your "amenities" offered to group leaders. Check with the ships' group coordinator by phone the next day after boarding to confirm your cocktail party and get confirmation as to exact time and place.

I prefer to have the party at 4:00 or 5:00pm on the last day of sailing. By the way, the last evening on board is never a "formal" dinner. The cocktail party gives me a chance to talk to my group about where to meet the last morning, a preview of the disembarkation procedures and what to expect going through U.S. immigration and customs.

The party also gives me the chance to make sure everyone in my group has the correct disembarkation tag to put on their checked bags. Special colored and numbered tags (Purple 3, for example) are given out to groups to enable them to leave the ship as a group. However, I have seen the ship give out the wrong tags to members of my group, so the party gives me a chance to make sure we all have the right tags.

I mentioned above, the term "amenities". Most cruise lines offer amenity points which are generally determined by the cruise destination. When you initially book the cruise for a group, the agent or their online system will tell you the number of amenity points you will have earned. The number is usually between 4 and 8 points.

For example, a bottle of champagne in each cabin might take 2 points, chocolate covered strawberries might take 1 or 2 points, a cocktail party with dry snacks might be another 2 points while a cocktail party with hot hors d'oeuvre's might require 4 points. If you have just 6 points to spend, it gets kind of tricky because you can't buy any more points.

After our first few cruises, I usually chose champagne in their cabin plus a cocktail party with dry snacks. The chilled champagne in their cabins upon arrival was always a big hit. I quickly learned that since we were having the cocktail party just before dinner, the hot snacks were hardly eaten and I had wasted some amenity points on that choice.

Most cruise lines require that the amenities be chosen prior to final payment time.

A note about cruise terminology: cruise vessels are called "ships" not "boats". An easy way to remember is a saying I'm told is taught in the Navy – "you can put a boat on a ship, but you can't put a ship on a boat". If the vessel carries several hundred or several thousand passengers, it's a ship. If it is small and operates primarily on rivers or just off shore, it's a boat.

I have a little fun with ship terminology on the bus on the way to the pier. I first tell them that they need to know the difference between "port" and "starboard". The easy way to remember is that port and left both have four letters. That leaves starboard as the right side. I even remind them that you must be facing forward to identify the sides of the ship.

I then tell them there are two more "nautical" terms they need to know. The front of the ship is known as the "pointy end" and the rear of the ship is referred to as the "roundy end". This always gets a laugh and they will use these terms to get a chuckle during the cruise.

Of course, the front of the ship is really the "bow" and the rear of the ship is known as the "stern".

Offering Overnight River Cruises

Overnight river cruises are quite different from ocean cruises. In many ways, river cruises are more like land tours since there is land on both sides of the boat and there is almost constant scenery and activity on the river. The river boats are much smaller than ocean-going ships and carry anywhere from 80 to 400 passengers with overnight cabins, lounges, dining facilities and friendly crews.

In the United States, there are fewer river boats operating in 2014 then there were a decade earlier. Hurricane Katrina had a devastating effect on the owners of river boats that traveled the Mississippi River and the downturn in the U.S. economy caused further problems.

For many years there were three river steamboats plying the Mississippi – the Delta Queen, the Mississippi Queen and the American Queen. These were all steam-powered paddle wheelers and offered cruises on the Mississippi as well as the Ohio and Missouri rivers. Today, of those three, only the American Queen is operating on those rivers, after some time out of service and a major refurbishing.

In addition to the three steamboats, Riverbarge Excursion Lines operated an overnight barge, the River Explorer, pushed by an historic towboat. The barge was actually two barges lashed together, with motel-size rooms on two levels on one barge and the dining room, lounge, showroom and passenger facilities on the other one.

On the River Explorer, shore excursions were included at stops along the way. We took a group on the River Explorer in 2003 from Memphis to Cincinnati upriver on both the Mississippi and Ohio rivers. It was a very good experience and we were disappointed that the company did not survive.

Unfortunately, the Riverbarge Company fell victim to the economic downturn of 2008 and went bankrupt. Last information about the River Explorer was that it was tied up in Port Arthur, Texas having been sold in August 2011 at government auction. We hope now that the economy is improving it will be put back into service.

We took groups on the Mississippi Queen in 1997, and over Thanksgiving in 2005 and 2006. Little did we know as we stepped off the MQ in November, 2006, that we were to be the last passengers to sail on that steamboat. She was used as a hotel for government workers in New Orleans during the aftermath of Hurricane Katrina and then, sadly, was cut up for scrap.

The Delta Queen was built in 1926 in the Sacramento Delta area of California and later operated for many years on the Mississippi River. The steamboat operated during its last years under a special congressional exemption from the maritime laws which forbid a wooden superstructure (that part of the boat above the steel hull). Congress, in 2008, failed to pass another exemption for the Delta Queen and it was sold to become a bed and breakfast in Chattanooga, Tennessee.

At the time of this writing, the American Queen, built in 1996, after several years of non-use, has come back into service under the new American Queen Steamboat Company and offers 222 cabins and suites with a capacity of 432 passengers. Because the AQ just returned to service in 2013, the cabins are booked far in advance and it is difficult to get and hold group space.

A new boat, the Queen of the Mississippi is a smaller non-steam powered paddle wheeler owned by American Cruise Lines and is able to carry 150 overnight passengers. It operates primarily on the Mississippi River.

American Cruise Lines' 2014 small-ship cruise itineraries for their six river boats include Mississippi River cruises, Pacific Northwest cruises, New England, Mid-Atlantic and Southeast U.S. cruises ranging from 7 to 14 nights.

USA River Cruises, Blount Small Ship Adventures and others offer a wide-range of cruise opportunities to the client who wants to avoid flying overseas to begin a river cruise. As mentioned earlier, these small ship cruises are very informal and it is much easier to make new friends among the other passengers.

In 2004, we took a group on a very unique small ship cruise with American Canadian Caribbean Lines (now Blount Small Ship Adventures) from Warren, Rhode Island into New York harbor, up the Hudson River and into the Erie Canal. To my knowledge, Blount still has the only overnight ships that can traverse the Erie Canal with its low bridges and locks.

We were on the Grand Caribe with a capacity of 88 passengers. After three days on the Erie Canal with several stops along the way, we entered Lake Ontario and followed the New York coastline into the Saint Lawrence Seaway and visited Montreal and Quebec City before being bused back to our starting point. Our travelers thought it was a great cruise and have talked about it ever since.

The Details of Booking a River Cruise

The Erie Canal cruise required a significant amount of effort to make it work. I will use this cruise as an example of what had to be done in advance to plan it, price it and actually make it work for the 37 travelers that went with Patty and me.

First of all, I made the arrangements with the cruise line, then known as American Canadian Caribbean Lines (ACCL) to reserve a sufficient number of cabins to accommodate at least 40 passengers. The company has changed its name to Blount Small Ship Adventures, in honor of their late founder, Luther Blount.

On the small ship, the Grande Caribe, which has a total passenger capacity of 88, I had to choose from three different categories and three different prices to get twenty cabins. All the cabins had an outside window but they were of different sizes and were on different decks. Usually, the higher the deck the higher the price for the cabin.

Having three different choices for our guests is OK, because on ocean cruises I always offer three different categories of cabins; inside (no window), outside (window) and balcony (sliding glass door to a balcony).

Since ACCL does not handle air arrangements, I next contacted several airlines to price travel from either Las Vegas (150 miles away) or Phoenix (200 miles away) to our final destination in Providence, Rhode Island. Based on price and connections, I chose Southwest Airlines with an 8:20am flight out of Phoenix nonstop to Providence arriving at 4:20pm.

Now that I had reservations for a cruise and roundtrip air, I needed to make arrangements for hotel rooms in both Phoenix and Providence. Making hotel reservations needs to be done before you can ask for quotes from charter bus companies.

I called a hotel near the Phoenix airport that I had used several times before, found the rates were still reasonable and made reservations for our departure date and for our return date.

I should re-state at this point that our policy has always been that on the flight coming home, if we can't get our travelers back to Lake Havasu City before 9:00pm, we will overnight and bring them back the next day rested and happy.

Next, I called the cruise line, ACCL, located in Warren, Rhode Island, for their suggestion on a hotel relatively close to their dock, and was given the suggestion of Johnson & Wales Inn in nearby Seekonk, Massachusetts. For a westerner, it seemed strange to overnight in another state, but it was only about six miles from the ship in Warren, Rhode Island.

The Johnson & Wales Inn turned out to be an excellent suggestion, because, not only was the hotel very impressive, but even more impressive was the fact that it was operated by Johnson and Wales University as a teaching hotel and was staffed by students. This was an experience that our travelers truly enjoyed.

I made reservations at the Johnson and Wales Inn for the night before our cruise departure and for the night that we were bused back to the Providence area from Quebec City before our flight home.

Now that I had hotels reserved, I needed to arrange bus transportation from Lake Havasu City to and from the Phoenix airport as well as to and from the Johnson and Wales Inn and the Providence airport. We needed to leave Lake Havasu City two days before the 2:00pm departure of the cruise to be there on time.

Upon arrival in Providence, I needed another charter bus to take us from the airport to the hotel where we were staying for the night. Again, I asked the cruise line for a suggestion on a charter bus company, which they were happy to provide, and made arrangements for a hotel to airport transfer after our cruise.

Dealing with a hotel and bus company that has been recommended by the cruise company gives greater assurance that you will receive a fair price and reliable service since they want to receive continued referrals from the cruise personnel.

In addition to reserving rooms with the two hotels, I needed to make meal reservations. At this point it is important to understand that for this type of trip it is beneficial to have hotels that also have restaurant and banquet facilities. Without these facilities, it would require that you pay for a bus to move your group to a restaurant and back at additional cost.

Both the Fiesta Inn in Tempe (near the Phoenix airport) and Johnson and Wales (near Providence, Rhode Island) have excellent banquet facilities and were easy to work with for the needs of my group.

At our banquets at Johnson & Wales Inn, we were served by students in tuxedos with a student maitre d' in charge. This was very impressive to our group of senior adults!

You can see that making arrangements for a river cruise is very detailed, and required a significant amount of time on the telephone and with email contacts to make reservations for the following:

- The cruise, with confirmed dates and time of arrival and departure
- Group air arrangements (compare rates and schedules between Las Vegas and Phoenix, then make a decision)
- Hotels in Phoenix and Providence reasonably close to the airports
- Dinner and breakfast in the hotels in Phoenix and Providence
- Bus service from Lake Havasu City to the Phoenix area hotel
- Bus service the next morning from the hotel to the Phoenix airport
- Bus service from the Providence airport to Johnson and Wales Inn
- Bus service the next morning from the hotel to the ACCL dock
- Bus service from Quebec City to our hotel was included in the cruise price and arranged by the cruise company
- Bus service the next morning from Johnson and Wales to the Providence airport
- Bus service from the Phoenix airport to our Phoenix area hotel
- Bus service the next morning from Phoenix to Lake Havasu City

When all of the arrangements are made and thoroughly checked, then checked again, the end result is a tour or cruise that is made to look easy and effortless. The traveler goes away with great memories and is the recipient of a terrific cruise "experience".

See Figure 39 for a copy of the profit projection spreadsheet for our Erie Canal cruise in 2004.

Be aware that the prices shown were for 2004 and prices for the same cruise and accommodations today would certainly be higher.

Comparing Ocean and River Cruises

River cruising is much less "glamorous" than sailing on a big ocean liner. The total number of passengers on board will range from 50 to as many as 400. The cabins are smaller and usually without a television (which is OK because you'll want to be watching the shorelines instead). Most cabins are outside with windows that usually can be opened or the cabin will have a balcony.

The boat may have occasional entertainment on board but often they will bring in local musical groups to entertain from the local village or town where you are tied up for the night. Speakers are often scheduled to inform you about the river, the locks system or the history of the surrounding region.

River boat meals are served in the dining room generally with open seating. Open seating means that you are not seated with your group but will sit wherever there is space when you enter the dining room, and you will have the opportunity to get to know your fellow travelers. This actually works very well.

The biggest difference between river and ocean cruises is that traveling on a river, there is usually land within sight on both sides of the boat. There is no time "at sea", where all you see is water. You are able to see towns, farms, wildlife and activity all along your route. You will often see other river boats along the way as well as commercial barges and private recreational boats.

On a river cruise, you won't want to take a nap during the day because you might miss something. If the cruise is in Europe, you need to be ever watchful for the many castles that line the rivers. Actually, on our cruise, the captain or the cruise director would announce each castle as it came into view.

River boats often stop along the way for shore excursions to see historic towns or structures or to visit an actual working farm. On many river cruises, the shore excursions are included in the cost of the cruise, so buses pull in and everybody gets on.

At night, the boat would tie up in a village or small town, often giving guests the opportunity to walk through the downtown and meet the locals or visit a pub. To summarize, river boat travel is very casual with ample opportunity to get to know your fellow travelers and the chance to follow the original "water highways" where history was made a century or more earlier.

In comparison, ocean cruises are taken on much larger vessels usually holding as few as 680 passengers (Princess Cruises' *Ocean Princess* and three ships from Oceania) to as many as 5,400 passengers (Royal Caribbean's *Oasis of the Seas)*. As a general rule, big ships have more features, more amenities and cost somewhat less.

Ocean cruises sail from major coastal cities to well-known ports-of-call with first-class entertainment each evening, luxurious surroundings, and never-ending activities. Smaller ships tend to offer cozier, more community-like atmosphere at a somewhat higher price.

We have had great experiences on both small and large ships and I encourage you to offer some of each type when your business and its following of travelers become large enough.

Most river cruise lines will not make air arrangements for your group. This means that you will have to deal with the groups department of the airlines that offer service to the cruise starting point and make your own arrangements.

Booking a group of 40-50 travelers on an airline can get complex. First, several of the airlines will give you a low price for the first batch of seats (maybe twenty) in your group. Then, the next ten seats, for instance, will carry a higher price and the next ten an even higher price for the flight.

Obviously, you don't want to advertise several prices for your river cruise because of different air rates, so I have always picked the number of travelers that I thought I had a reasonable chance of selling, calculated the total cost of the various air rates and taxes for that number, and then divided the total cost by the number of travelers to arrive at an average airfare price. I would then use this figure to calculate the total price of the cruise.

Of course, other factors such as overnight stays before and after the cruise, bus charters to and from the airport and to and from the river boat, meals that you will provide along the way and luggage handling need to be figured into the offering price. Working with the *Excel* spreadsheet discussed earlier enables you to come up with a total cost for the cruise and a reasonable return for your effort.

Escorting a Major Tour

I've defined a "major tour" in this book as a tour contracted by you with a large, nation-wide or world-wide tour company. This would be a method for offering a tour outside of your geographical comfort zone.

In our case, we considered our geographical comfort zone to be the Western states of Arizona, California, New Mexico, Nevada, Southern Utah and Southern Colorado. In these areas, we could design and scout a tour in our personal vehicle without flying. We also considered that we could conduct these tours all by bus from our Lake Havasu City starting point.

When we chose to do a tour outside of this area, we would choose a tour from a large, reputable company such as Collette Vacations, Globus, Trafalgar, Perillo Tours and others. Once we chose the tour we would begin marketing it along with the others that we were offering.

Escorting a tour being conducted by another company is quite different from escorting your own tour. Let's use a tour to Italy as an example with the tour beginning in Rome and ending in Milan. The tour manager will be meeting us in Rome and leaving us in Milan.

You will act as the tour manager/escort from the time you leave home until you arrive at the Rome Airport and are met by the large company tour manager.

For instance, if you travel by bus from your home area to the airport, you will be instructing your guests about the airport and how to stay together at any other airports you will be stopping in before arriving in Rome. In many cases, because of our distance from an airport, an overnight was necessary near the airport before the morning flight.

If you have a nearby airport where everyone can meet, you will be in charge of keeping the group together during initial check-in, any change of planes, and final arrival in Rome.

It is very important to realize that as soon as the large company tour manager meets the group at the final airport, he or she is in charge!

I made sure to tell my travelers that once we were joined by the tour manager, I would become one of the group. I told them that I would not know anything more about tomorrow's itinerary than what had been announced to the group or was in an itinerary that the tour manager had provided to everyone.

You will be escorting the group, but all questions from your group should be directed to the tour manager. In fact, the first thing I told the tour manager when we met at the airport was that it was their tour and I wanted them to run the tour just as they would any other tour made up of individuals. I explained that Patty and I would be happy to help, but only if he or she asked for our help.

Remember, this professional tour manager is used to leading a group alone.

Even though they don't need your help, if, for instance, on the first day of the tour someone is late getting back to the bus, the tour manager may call on you to find them and bring them to the bus simply because you probably know who you are looking for and the tour manager can be talking to the group while you're gone.

The worst thing you can do is to ask the tour manager to change the itinerary because you have read about some site along the way that they have not included in their itinerary. Changing the itinerary on the fly is a recipe for trouble.

Respect the tour manager and the company by accepting the tour exactly as they have designed it. If you feel strongly about adding something, contact the company months in advance of the tour to see if it can be done.

You may find, as I have, that the tour manager is so pleased that they don't have to spend time explaining to you why they can't change the itinerary that they will sometimes suggest something extra that is not in the standard itinerary but is on the tour route.

When the tour is over and the tour manager says goodbye at the airport, you must be ready to take charge of the group again and deal with any issues that may come up on your way home. Remember, a good part of your group would not have had the courage to do this far-away tour on their own and you are their "security" to take care of everything for them.

On occasion, the tour manager may be flying back to the states on the same flight with you and your guests. Respect the fact that the tour manager is now on his or her own time. Make sure you make it clear to your guests that the tour manager's duties are over and that they are not to be bothered. Our experience has been that tour managers are very good at sleeping all the way on long flights.

Offering Travel Insurance

Before you begin to offer major tours and cruises, you will want to make arrangements to offer travel insurance to your travelers. Travel insurance protects your guests from a monetary loss due to injury or illness before your departure or during the tour or cruise.

When you are ready to offer travel insurance, Google "travel insurance companies" and contact two or three about their requirements for their agents. In most states, a "limited" insurance license is required and can be obtained from the state insurance department.

In Arizona, no classes or tests are required to obtain the "limited" license to sell travel insurance. The license is valid for four years and currently costs $50 to renew. The travel insurance company will not allow you to sell their products until they have a copy of your license.

I was an agent for several travel insurance companies, but I sold Travel Guard Insurance for about the last ten years. Their service was very good and they never refused a claim.

Their agent commission, if the application was completed online (by either the traveler or me), was 20% of the total premium. The total of my commissions for the sale of travel insurance was generally $2,000 to $3,000 per year, a figure that went right to the bottom line.

I did not offer travel insurance on the tours that we designed and conducted ourselves. If someone had a valid reason for cancelling, even at a late date, I refunded everything that I could get back from hotels, restaurants and attractions.

If I was not able to get all reservations refunded, I sent them the amount I was able to get back along with a letter of explanation. This was a part of my Terms and Conditions document that was sent to all travelers on their first tour with us.

See Figure 20 for our Terms and Conditions (referred to earlier).

Cruise lines and large tour companies have very strict cancellation rules. Up until final payment time, the deposit is usually fully refundable. After final payment time, the amount of refund depends on when the cruise line is given notice of the cancellation.

Generally, the refund amount will go to 75% of the full payment after final payment time, then later will ratchet down to 50%, then 25%, and for the last 60 days it will likely be 0% or totally non-refundable.

When you determine what the exact refund policy is from the cruise line or tour company, make sure it is spelled out in the confirmation that you will send at reservation time and in your final invoice to the traveler.

To protect against the possible loss of their travel investment, most travelers choose to buy travel insurance that will reimburse them for the part that the cruise line or tour company does not reimburse, thus returning a total of 100% of what they have paid for the vacation.

Let me be clear. The travel insurance will not reimburse your guest if they decide at the last moment that they have the sniffles or that they have a family gathering during the time of the cruise. The reason for cancellation must be for something that has happened to them after they made final payment and is serious enough that they are unable to travel or their doctor has advised them not to travel.

It is extremely important that you explain to your guests in writing about non-refundable dates and that travel insurance is available to protect their travel investment. Without travel insurance, make sure they understand that they are "self insuring" and that there are no exceptions.

Travel insurance is like any other type of insurance. You can't wait until after your house burns down to buy fire insurance. In the same way, your guests can't wait until they break a leg or have the flu to decide to buy travel insurance.

It is important to make sure your travelers understand they are not buying medical insurance. Most policies will cover any unreimbursed medical expenses, but the main object of travel insurance is to cover against an unforeseen accident or illness that makes it impossible for them to travel or any accident or illness they might suffer while traveling.

To make sure your guest will be able to get a claim approved from the travel insurance company, it is imperative that they visit a doctor immediately and explain to the doctor that he or she will be signing their name to a travel insurance document stating that the guest is unable to travel or has been advised not to travel.

If the person who must cancel intended to travel with a spouse or a friend, and they both purchased travel insurance, the other person can choose to go on the tour or cruise and have the insurance company pay the single-supplement charge, or they can choose to cancel and receive a refund in the same manner as the guest who is unable to travel.

Most travel insurance extends to immediate family members as well. Some years ago, an adult daughter of a man who was scheduled to travel with us was admitted to a mental hospital just before our trip was to leave. Naturally, he wanted to be with his daughter and was relieved to know that his travel insurance would cover him and reimburse the amount he had paid for the cruise.

What is stated above about travel insurance rules and policies are as they were in 2012, when I sold my tour business. Make sure you clearly understand all the terms and conditions of any insurance that you are selling or representing. Your travelers will ask you for advice about buying insurance, but in most cases you should pass on that advice.

When asked, "Do you think I should buy travel insurance?", my response was usually, "Do you have fire insurance on your home?" When they say, "Yes, of course", I would usually say, "Travel insurance is the same thing. You buy it hoping never to use it."

On the last few overseas tours and cruises we offered, I required that our travelers purchase travel insurance. For one thing, Medicare coverage is not valid outside of the United States. Another reason is that if you need to be returned to the U.S. for treatment, in most cases, travel insurance will cover the cost of your travel home and reimburse you for the unused portion of your vacation.

Most travel insurance companies offer several levels of coverage, such as "Gold", "Silver" and "Basic". I never wanted to make things too difficult for my travelers, so I chose to offer a single plan that gave adequate coverage at a reasonable price.

This plan was usually the middle, or "Silver", plan. This would be the only plan I would offer, but, in rare cases when someone inquired about a better plan, I would then send them information on the more expensive plan for their consideration. This seldom happened.

Most of the larger tour companies offer insurance plans as well. They usually are quite competitively priced and offer good features. The big problem for a tour operator is that they only cover the cost of their tour.

In our case, being remote from an airport, our package price included the bus transportation to the airport and home, a possible overnight stay at one or both ends of the trip, meals, etc. These extra costs would not be refundable from the tour company insurance plan. This made this type of plan unusable for our situation.

If your location is remote from an airport, where you provide bus transportation to the airport, you will want to offer an insurance plan that covers the entire price of your packaged tour.

If you decide to offer the tour company's plan, (one that will only reimburse what has been paid to the large tour company, not your total price), be sure you state in writing what that plan covers and what it does not, so that you don't end up with customers who feel that they should get a full refund.

Be aware, that if you offer the insurance that the large tour company or the cruise line offers, your customer that has to cancel may expect a full reimbursement. If they only get that portion that the tour company or cruise line was paid, they may naturally believe that you will reimburse the rest of what they paid you.

For the reasons above, I did not ever offer any travel insurance that did not cover the entire price of the tour or cruise. I recommend that you do the same and offer a plan that covers the complete cost of the travel package.

Setting up Office Procedures

I stated in the earlier chapter, "Basic Ingredients for Success as a Tour Operator", that a good customer records system as well as a good accounting system is a must to assure your success in this business. You may be thinking that you just want to travel and make money leading tours, but I have to tell you that without keeping close track of your customers and your money, you cannot be successful.

If this sounds distasteful to you, then you probably should just form a loosely organized travel club and be satisfied with organizing tours among your friends and getting to go free, or at a reduced rate, for your efforts.

The Need for a Computer

Although someone might be able to operate a very small tour operation without a computer, I can't imagine why anyone would want to. You will see in this chapter that almost all of what you need to do to plan, organize and conduct a tour will be done on a computer. I prefer a desk computer but a laptop could perform all the functions necessary. The basic tasks you will need to perform and the most popular programs available are as follows:

> Internet Searches – *Internet Explorer* or similar search engine
> Email – Microsoft *Outlook**
> Word Processing – Microsoft *Word**
> Spreadsheets – Microsoft *Excel**
> Publishing – Microsoft *Publisher*
> Accounting – *Quicken*
> Customer Records – Lotus *Approach***
> Mapping – Microsoft *Streets & Trips*

> *Currently sold as a part of Microsoft Office Small Business pkg for about $200.
> **Available online as Lotus SmartSuite Millennium Edition V 9.8.1 for under $30.

Internet

The Internet is a very important tool that you can use to assist in planning tours, finding possible hotels and restaurants and checking out attractions along the way.

To perform searches you will want to use a "search engine" such as Google or Yahoo. You will soon learn how to ask the right question to bring up answers you can use. I have mentioned earlier using the Internet to search for interesting background on the areas you will be visiting so that you can add that to your tour commentary.

In addition to using the Internet to find useful information, you will want to use it to help potential travelers find your business. This means you will need a website. There are website tools you can use to design your own, you can have a friend design and maintain it (as I did), or you can contract with a website designer to build it for you. Above all, your website needs to reflect a professional image of your business.

When people come to your website you want them to be able to learn about you as the owners and escorts; they need to be able to see your tour schedule, learn the date and price and read details about each tour, and read testimonials from satisfied travelers. Of course, you want them to get excited about one or more tours and be able to sign up online, email you or call you as a result of viewing your website.

My website was designed by a high school friend who enjoyed being creative with his computer. It consisted of a home page with a picture of Patty and me and a short history of our business. From the home page, the guest could easily navigate to our tour schedule, to the "About Us" page, to a contacts page, to a travel insurance page and to a testimonials page.

See Figure 1 (referred to earlier) for sample pages from our website.

166

Email

Email is an absolute must in today's business environment. Although you may make initial contact by telephone with a new charter bus company, a hotel or a restaurant, later confirmations will most likely be sent by email, not by US mail. Email is used for most business communications where you want and need a written quote, confirmation or contract.

In addition to sending business communications as mentioned above, you will want to occasionally email information to your travelers and potential travelers about upcoming tours, price changes, and other news of interest.

Word Processing

Even though you will use email for most business correspondence, you will probably find out that not everyone who wants to travel with you will be using Email. I found that mailing the final invoice along with a detailed information sheet to everyone going on a particular tour was the best way. All these printed pages have to be done on a computer with a word processing program such as Microsoft *Word*. If you are not familiar with *Word*, there are online tutorials to help you become proficient. Once you have produced the "master" copy, additional copies can be printed on your computer printer or taken to a copy shop for less expensive copies.

Spreadsheets

I have mentioned spreadsheets earlier in this book, but I want to emphasize here, that they are vital to the tour business. A spreadsheet program, such as Microsoft *Excel*, makes simple work of listing all the costs of a tour and determining a price based on an estimated number of participants.

A spreadsheet program also makes it possible to determine your breakeven point – that point with x number of travelers at which you just break even (income equals expenses therefore there is no profit or loss). In the early days of your tour business you may want to go ahead with a tour, even without a profit, to build your reputation.

Actually, it's more likely that you will use the spreadsheet to determine the lowest number of passengers you can take to make an acceptable profit. With a spreadsheet program like Microsoft *Excel*, you can see different results in seconds by just changing the one number representing the number of travelers.

Publishing

Publishing is the term used for a program that will allow you to make flyers, announcements, invitations and brochures.

I used Microsoft Publisher to lay out my 4-page tour brochure before I took it to a local printer. I laid out each page, wrote all the tour descriptions, wrote an "editorial" message and inserted the necessary disclaimers. When I thought it was correct, I let Patty proofread it and she always found some changes that needed to be made. I'll explain more about our brochure later.

In addition to using Publisher for our brochure, I often used it to make up flyers for major tours and cruises. When someone called about these offerings, I would mail or email the flyer, a detailed day-by-day itinerary and an insurance brochure.

See Figure 36 for an example of a cruise flyer (referred to earlier).

Accounting

The good news is that the accounting for a tour business is rather simple compared to a retail store or a small manufacturer. Most businesses have Accounts Receivable (money owed to the business for products or services already delivered); Accounts Payable (money that the business owes for supplies and raw materials already received); and Payroll (money owed to employees less deductions for withholding taxes, insurance, etc).

In a small tour business, your travelers will be paying at least 30 days in advance of each tour, so there is no Accounts Receivable. Most of the tour expenses will be paid before or during the tour, therefore, no Accounts Payable to keep track of. And, if your business is to be like ours, where we operated the business without employees, there is no payroll.

Quicken is a program available for simple personal or business accounting. It allows you to keep track of all income plus checks written to pay all expenses either paid directly or through a credit card.

Quicken allows you to categorize income between tour revenue, per tour and cruise commissions, per cruise. Expenses can be categorized between office supplies, membership dues, automobile and other incidentals, but the majority will be distributed to "Tour Expense". Cash expenses can also be handled and assigned to a particular tour or to other business expenses.

Quicken allows you to distribute each item of income and expense to a category.

The categories I used in our business were as follows:

INCOME

- Tour Revenue
- Cruise Commissions
- Travel Insurance Commissions

EXPENSES

- Advertising & Promotion
- Auto
- Bank Charges
- Charitable Donations
- Computer Assistance
- Dues for Clubs & Organizations
- Insurance, Liability
- Legal and Accounting Fees
- License Fees
- Office
- Office Rent
- Phone
- Postage
- Scouting Travel
- Supplies
- Tour Expenses (by far the largest category)
- Website

Quicken also allows you to split out a category such as "Tour Expenses" to the individual tour. Quicken calls these breakouts "tags". So, within the category of "Tour Expenses", I set up tags for each tour code as I began to have charges for a particular tour. This made it possible to record all tour expenses for a tour code such as "PS10" and then produce an Income & Expense report for that Palm Springs tour.

Bartlett Tours was incorporated as a "C" corporation, but if you choose an "S" corporation or a Limited Liability Company (LLC), there may also be additional expense items for salaries, profit sharing, Social Security, and business income taxes. Please be sure to consult with your accountant about the best way to organize your business and what expense items you will need to account for.

A business credit card is the easiest way to pay for expenses before, during and after the tour and gives you a complete record. Hotels, restaurants and even charter bus companies are very happy to accept a business credit card as payment. When you receive your credit card statement each month, you enter the total amount of the payment in Quicken, and then distribute each individual charge to the appropriate category and tag.

I chose not to keep track of every incoming check by tag (tour code), because of the volume of checks coming in for up to 15 different tours. However, when the tour was over, I calculated the exact revenue for the tour and put a tag on the total amount that was revenue directly from that tour.

Quicken allows you to pull a report almost immediately after the tour's ending that will show you all the revenue and expenses for that tour and more importantly, the net total profit for the tour. QuickBooks is another program for more complex accounting needs, but in my opinion, it is not needed in a small tour business.

I just recently upgraded to Quicken Home and Business 2014. It has all the features of the "plain" Quicken, but it does provide some features on the business side that might be advantageous to you. I chose the "Home and Business" version because I am the treasurer of a business "leads" club and decided it provided reports that would be important to the officers and board of directors of my club.

Customer Records

Keeping accurate customer records is vital to the success of your tour business. It is important to capture the name(s), home address and email address and phone number of anyone who calls or contacts you with an inquiry about a tour. Each caller is added to your mailing list for future tour announcements. It is cost saving to email your information, but if you have a professional looking printed brochure, I feel it makes a better impression on the new prospect if you mail them one.

In our tour business, many of our travelers were "snowbirds" or winter residents in our area. In that case, I always got both summer and winter addresses so that I could mail updates or changes in any month. Of course, with most people having email that they can receive wherever they are, a second address is less important.

My record for each individual or married couple included their preferred name (i.e. "Bill") as well as their given or legal name (i.e. "William"). The legal name is needed for any touring with a large tour company or overseas travel where a passport is required. This is not information that you would ask for on the first contact, but the record needs to have space for it so it can be added as needed.

In addition to space on the customer record for preferred and given names, one or more addresses, telephone numbers, and email address, my record also had space for a listing of tours actually taken with us and notes about the guest. Notes might include the name of a daughter that traveled with the guest, a disability, the date of death of a spouse, or anything else that would be pertinent to view in the future.

See Figure 40 and Figure 41 for screenshots of my individual customer records using Lotus *Approach*.

Because we were fortunate enough to have guests that traveled on 20, 30, 40 or as many as 60 tours with us, I devised a simple code to identify each tour, both for the customer record as well as for identifying a particular tour within Quicken. The code was two letters for the name of the tour and two numbers for the year of the tour.

For instance, a tour to Tucson and Southern Arizona in 2011 was coded "TU11". A Christmas Musical Shows Tour in 2010 was coded CH10. Occasionally, there can be a conflict in codes, as for instance, when we toured China in 2006. "CH" was already taken for our Christmas musical shows tours, so I had to invent another code for China. Since the tour included a 4-day cruise on the Yangtze River, I coded that tour "YR06".

The important thing is that the code needs to be one that you can readily recognize when you see it on the customer record. However, at the end of 19 years worth of codes, I sometimes had to refer to a list of codes that I maintained to refresh my memory.

Tours that we repeated used the same letters for the tour with a different set of numbers for the year. For instance, we repeated the Christmas Musical Shows Tour into Southern California several times, so the tour codes were CH01, CH02, CH05, CH07, CH09, and CH10.

The Palm Springs Follies was the only tour that we ever did more than once in a year. This was so popular, that in 2009 and 2010 we did an overnight tour in both February and March. In that instance, I added an "F" for February and an "M" for March. This made the codes "PS09F" and "PS09M". As I mentioned earlier, I used the same codes to identify those expenses that were to be charged to a particular tour.

There are multiple uses for the data you will have in your customer records. These include:
- Name and address mailing labels for brochures & envelopes
- Name labels for affixing to plastic guest badges – See Figure 24
- Last Name Only labels for luggage tags & boarding passes – See Figure 25
- Tour Manifest (list of those going on the tour) – See Figure 28
- Searches by tour, by name, or by date of record creation*
- *By recording the year someone asks to be on your mailing list, you can choose to send a mailing or drop them if it has been several years and they have taken no tours

Name and address mailing labels: This use of the customer records program simplifies sending a mailing to all on your list or, by selectively searching, for just those that meet particular criteria. For instance, if I wanted to send information to only those that had signed up to go with us on our next Tucson tour, I would search the tours field for "TU13" and then select a button for "labels".

However, if I were mailing a new brochure, I might select all of those in customer records or, I might select based on the years since their last tour with us, to send only to those that had traveled with us in the last 3 years. If the same brochure could be emailed, I might select to pay postage only for those for whom I did not have an email address.

If I were doing a group mailing, I used sheets with thirty 1" x 2 5/8" labels per page and printed them on my printer. However, for doing one label, there is a single label machine made by Brother that can be attached to your computer to produce single labels.

I never sent out any mail without a printed address label. This way it forced me to enter the new prospects name and address into my computer right after the contact and kept me from forgetting to enter it.

Name labels for affixing to plastic guest badges: When we first started our tour business, we printed name tags that could fit into clear plastic holders that could be pinned to our guests' shirts. As we became more established, I wanted something that looked more professional.

I was able to order plastic badges that were the same size as a credit card with our Bartlett Tours logo and a rectangular box for the name label. These plastic badges cost about 22 cents each when ordered from the "Signatures" company in a quantity of 2,000. The badges worked very well and the new owners of our company are still using the same badge today.

See Figure 23 (referred to earlier) for a look at our name tags, boarding passes and luggage tags.

I special ordered a bright pink or "hot pink" tag with strings attached for our luggage tags. They were highly visible and when having Sky Caps pull luggage off of airport carousels, I would show them a tag I always carried and they knew exactly which bags were ours.

You notice I said to order the tags _with strings attached_. These tags are special orders that I got through my local office supply. One time, the order was sent without the request for "strings attached". When the order came in, the elastic strings were packed separately from the 1,000 luggage tags. Guess who got to put the string on all 1,000 tags?

What program was I using for Customer Records? From 1993 until I sold Bartlett Tours in 2012, I used a database program known as Lotus _Approach_, version 9.8.1. I would recommend that you use Lotus _Approach_, but you need to be aware that it has not been updated for several years and IBM, who acquired Lotus in 1995, announced in 2013 that they would no longer provide technical support.

That may seem like a big problem, but I can report that I have not had a single time in 19 years when the program failed me and I needed support. The new owners of my tour company continue to use Lotus _Approach_ without any problems.

However, there is another consideration with choosing Lotus Approach. It will run without a problem on Windows 7, 32 bit, but not when Windows 7 is configured for 64 bit. I have been running Approach under Windows 7, 32 bit for over three years without a problem. My understanding is that Approach will not operate under Windows 8, which may or may not present a problem to a new business. My guess is that Windows 7 will be around for another 8-10 years.

At the time of this writing in 2014, I found Lotus SmartSuite Millennium Edition 9.8, which includes _Approach_ available on Amazon.com for under $30. Other programs included with _Approach_ are their spreadsheet program, Lotus _1-2-3_ and their word processing program called Lotus _WordPro_. Even though I used both of these programs for twenty years, they have been replaced in the marketplace by Microsoft's _Excel_ and _Word_.

If you have concerns about using a discontinued product like _Approach_, which may limit the possibility of upgrading your computer to new Windows versions in the future, I suggest you look into the features of Microsoft _Access_, a database program that is current, but one that I am not familiar with. I am told that *Access* can manipulate customer records at least as well as Approach, but I have no experience with the *Access* product.

Mapping

Microsoft *Streets & Trips* seems to be the most popular mapping system and it is improved with new versions every few years. In the earlier chapter, *Preparing a Preliminary Tour Itinerary,* I explained the use of a mapping program in setting up and timing each tour itinerary. The more you use this program the more familiar with it you will become and the more valuable it will be to your tour operation. An online search found that the 2013 version is selling for less than $30.

See Figure 2 and Figure 3 for screenshots of *Streets & Trips (referred to earlier).*

Running your Office

Once again, I want to emphasize that owning and operating a tour business is not all about travel and having fun with your groups. You must run it like the business that it is. You will have to think about the business like a CEO (Chief Executive Officer), even if you are assigning tasks only to yourself. The tasks of running a tour business include the following:

TOUR PLANNING

- o Identifying future tour possibilities
- o Scouting new tours
- o Planning in some detail all tours for at least the next year
- o Making hotel reservations
- o Making meal reservations
- o Making charter bus reservations
- o Making reservations at all the attractions you will visit
- o Making sure you receive confirmations on all the above reservations
- o Accurately pricing each future tour
- o Making deposits to hotels, restaurants, etc. on time
- o Sending a rooming list to each hotel 30 days in advance of arrival
- o Making a local reservation for your driver the night before departure (if needed)

PROMOTING AND ADVERTISING YOUR TOURS

- o Mailing and/or emailing a brochure at least twice each year
- o Advertising in local newspapers, shoppers, etc
- o Maintaining a website that is accurate and user friendly
- o Emailing occasional "alerts" or updates in between mailings
- o Belonging to community organizations (Rotary, Elks, Chamber of Commerce, etc)

CUSTOMER RELATED

- o Answering phone and email inquiries in a timely manner
- o Entering new inquiries into your Customer Records system
- o Mailing brochures to new prospects

- Taking and recording customer reservations
- Accurately recording deposits as they come in
- Confirming customer reservations
- Entering the tour code into the individual customer records system
- Mailing or emailing final invoices and final information for each tour
- Receiving and recording final payments
- Handling cancellations and refunding deposits to guests unable to travel

PREPARING FOR THE TOUR

- Preparing badges, luggage tags and boarding passes
- Preparing the detailed itinerary for the next tour for the driver and yourself
- Preparing the itinerary for the tour for your guests
- Preparing final name lists for the tour to hand to your guests
- Making sure that water and snacks are ready for the tour
- Getting sufficient cash for cash tips along the way
- Preparing a seating chart if your tour is to a theatre performance (Assign the best seats, in order, to those who signed up first)

OTHER NECESSARY OFFICE DUTIES

- Paying monthly bills for utilities, insurance, advertising, etc.

Obviously, the items above are not necessarily done in that order. When you are getting ready for a tour that leaves tomorrow, the phone will still ring with new reservations for upcoming tours, mail will arrive with things that need to be done now, and deposits will be due on future tours. I used a checklist during the last week before a tour to make sure that everything was thought of and completed.

See Figure 22 to review my Checklist (referred to earlier).

I chose never to take office work with me on a tour. In fact, I didn't check email or phone messages during a tour. I left a message on my phone that said:

"Hello. You've reached Bartlett Tours. Our office will be closed from October 15th through the 19th while we are escorting a tour. Please leave a message and I'll call you back when I return".

178

I felt that I always wanted to give 100% of my attention to the tour I was conducting and to the guests we had on that tour. I never had a complaint from anyone who called and had to wait a few days for me to return their call. I think they understood and agreed with the attention I was paying to the current tour.

Most of the office tasks shown above were done on my computer. However, I chose to keep a binder on my desk for recording new reservations. I had a tab and three blank lined pages for each tour that had been announced and was available. This book was used to record the names of those who called, emailed or sent notice that they wanted to sign up for a particular tour.

I recorded the name in pen and made sure that I had the customer record for that person or couple on my computer. When I received the initial deposit, I went to that line in my book and wrote the amount of the deposit next to the name. I used two lines for a couple or for singles traveling together. The lines were numbered so that I could see at a glance how many reservations I had for each tour.

When I had a cancellation I would put a single line through the names in the book and write next to the deposit amounts, "ref 9/15/12", indicating the date the refund was sent. This helps when a guest calls and claims they have not received the refund. Rarely is it a problem with the mail. The envelope containing the refund check is usually lost in a stack of mail on the guest's counter at home.

When final payments were received, I entered them by pen on the same line in the Reservation Book. Only after all final payments were received did I enter the tour code (DV12) into the field in the Approach Customer Record for each person or couple. When I completed this data entry, I brought up a list of participants and checked that against the handwritten reservation forms.

I found that it's easier to work with a written record in a book rather than on the customer's computer record because of changes and cancellations that invariably happen over the weeks and months before the tour. This method also minimizes the chance that your final passenger list will show a person who cancelled but his or her customer record was not changed.

I found that if we offered one tour per month for nine or ten months each year, it provided a very good income and also left enough time to take care of the business end of our tour company. These months without a tour also allowed time to take necessary scouting trips.

Occasionally, we would schedule two tours in the same month if they were each 2-day or 3-day tours. Most of the effort of planning the next years' schedule was done during the months with no tours.

I should point out that our tour schedule was heavier in the winter months of October through March when our winter residents came to Arizona. Many of the winter residents wanted to be active during the winter and loved tours into California where many were afraid to drive on their own.

Summer tours were dependent on our year-round residents and tended to be shorter and into cooler areas. We often experience temperatures in Lake Havasu City during the summer of 110 degrees or higher for three to four months. But, don't feel sorry for us, "it's a dry heat".

During these slower months, you need to constantly think about ways to promote your business in your market area. If you are operating without employees, as we did, you need to coordinate your advertising so that you're not running an ad asking potential clients to call your number when you are away on tour.

Keeping Up with the Tour Industry

 You'll find that as your business begins to roll, you'll wonder what others in the tour industry are doing. A good way to keep abreast of the business is to subscribe to tour magazines.

Tour Magazines

Listed below are magazines that I have received over the years. When I was reading them, I paid particular attention to the advertisements for attractions that might be something that we would like to add to our schedule. Even if the particular business was out of our tour area, it might give me an idea of something similar that we could utilize.

The magazines below are listed in alphabetical order and provide a way to order a free subscription to each. In most cases, you can choose to receive a printed magazine or view the magazine online.

Bus Tours Magazine
National Bus Trader, Inc
www.bustoursmagazine.com

Destinations
The official publication of the American Bus Association
www.buses.org

Groups Today
Serendipity Media LLC
www.groupstoday.com

Group Travel Directory
Premier Tourism Marketing, Inc.
info@ptmgroups.com

Leisure Group Travel
Premier Travel Media
info@ptmgroups.com

If you talk with anyone when requesting a subscription to any of these magazines, be sure to indicate that you are starting a tour business and are a serious tour operator. Most will be happy to include you in their subscriber list because you are a potential buyer for their advertisers' products.

See Figure 42 to read a short article I was asked to write about my tour experience for *Groups Today* magazine, March/April, 2012.

Tour Associations

As a small, local tour operator, I never belonged to any of the national organizations. I remember checking into the National Tour Association (NTA) during my first year, but I was told I needed to be in business for at least three years before I was eligible for membership. I thought that was reasonable, to make sure their members were successful.

After being in business a year or two, I realized that, for me, there probably was no need to be a member of a national organization. I was advertising and drawing my tour customers from a very small area of western Arizona. If I didn't maintain a high standard of service and honest dealings, the word would soon get around. I didn't need a national group to monitor me; my local customers would do that.

There are three major tour associations in the United States. They are:

- United States Tour Operators Association
- National Tour Association
- American Bus Association

Feel free to check each one and make your own decision as to whether you would benefit from being a member of one or more of these groups.

Trade Shows and "Fam" Tours

Trade shows are large gatherings held at convention hotels and put on by major trade associations for the benefit of their members and others in the industry. They feature speakers on industry topics, workshops of interest to attendees and an exhibit hall with vendors showing their products or services to the attendees.

You generally do not have to be a member of the association to attend their trade show, but there will be an admission charge.

Tourist attractions in the area represented will have exhibits and personnel on hand to encourage you to bring your tours to their attraction. If these attractions are in the area that you intend to serve, spend some time with them and get us much information as possible.

Hotels and attractions will have booths and exhibits and will be handing out information about their destinations. There will be representatives on hand to answer questions and give you further information in hopes that you will later book a tour to their locality.

Large tour companies will have exhibits and representatives on hand to discuss partnering with you, the small operator, for tours outside your area. The information you can gain from attending a trade show can often be extremely valuable to you in growing your business in the second through fifth year.

A trend that is taking place right now is a trend toward smaller, regional trade shows, usually limited in scope to a state or region within a state.

The trade show at these regional events features exhibits and representatives of convention and visitors bureaus from towns and cities within the region as well as state and county tourism officials. Representatives from hotels and attractions set up booths and are ready and willing to extol the virtues of their properties. You can make excellent contacts as you visit the booths within a trade show.

These regional trade shows are sometimes preceded by a Fam tour". Fam is short for familiarization. This is usually a relatively short tour of three or four days, offered only to tour operators and travel agents at a preferential price per person, and often sponsored by a state tourism board.

The intent of the Fam tour, of course, is to show tour operators a part of the country that they have not yet considered for one of their company's tours. The object is to excite a few of the tour operators enough that they will schedule a tour to this area sometime in the next year. Be open to participating in a Fam tour if it is offered.

Since trade shows and Fam tours are intended for tour operators, you will have time to get to know people involved in the same business as you, but in different areas of the country. Participants are usually very willing to share about their business and how they are doing things. You will undoubtedly pick up some pointers on how to run your business and may also learn about new tours that will fit into your plan.

Patty and I have attended three or four trade shows and have found them of some value. Because our tour business was so localized, the shows we attended were in

Phoenix and Las Vegas and only one of those included a Fam tour into Northern Nevada and Western Utah.

Fam tours are also offered by most major tour companies. These type of Fam tours are not connected to a travel trade show but are offered to tour operators at a significantly reduced rate to introduce you to their company and the region they are touring.

These tours are very professionally conducted and several company representatives, such as District Sales Managers, are along on the tour. You can often make valuable contacts for the future.

We have found Fam tours with large tour companies to be of significant value and we encourage you to spend some money checking out major tours that you think you could sell to your clientele.

If your favorite large tour company isn't offering a Fam to the area you are most interested in, talk to your regional sales manager for the company and they will usually allow you to go on a regular tour at a reduced rate. Remember, the money spent on Fam tours is an investment in the future of your tour business.

Over the 19 years we had our tour business we went on Fam tours to the following destinations:

- England, Ireland, Scotland & Wales
- Portugal River Cruise
- Yellowstone & the Grand Tetons
- Canadian Rockies
- Alaska by Land
- Mexico's Copper Canyon
- South America (Chile, Argentina & Brazil)
- Nova Scotia and the Maritime Provinces of Canada
- Washington DC and Williamsburg
- Branson Musical Shows

- Glacier National Park
- Russia River Cruise

These Fam tours were offered to us by major tour companies and river cruise companies in an effort to sell their company and their products. In most cases, we took a group on the same tour or cruise the next year.

Conclusion

As I mentioned in the beginning of this book, when I sold my business in May, 2012, I wrote procedures for many of the activities that would need to be done by the new owners. I realized that procedures that I had developed and completed for every tour would not be intuitively obvious to the new owner, Mike, and that he would need something in writing to follow, at least until he got some experience.

During the first few months after the sale, I spent numerous long sessions with Mike to coach him on various aspects of the business and to familiarize him with the upcoming tour. When he bought the business, he also bought the tours that we had already published and advertised – a total of nine bus tours within the western states, plus an overseas tour to Australia and New Zealand, and a Mexican Riviera cruise from Los Angeles.

It was during this time that I decided that I should put my experience into a book and encourage other people to enter into this exciting business.

Since I was able to start my business in 1993 without the help of a book or a coach, making decisions on the fly as was required, I felt that if I took some of the mystery out of starting a tour business, people with a love for travel would be drawn to it.

I sincerely feel that the ideal age for someone to start a tour business is in their fifties. At this point in their lives, there is a maturity and a level of life experience that better equips them to instill confidence in their travelers and handle unexpected situations as they come up.

In addition, if a person in their fifties has been prudent with their money over 30 years of employment, they should have a reasonable nest-egg and at least a minimum retirement income to allow for a slow building of the profits from a tour business.

This is not to say that a younger person, with the "right stuff" couldn't get into the tour business. However, it might be more feasible for a younger person to start as a tour guide or tour manager for a large, established tour company. This would enable the younger person to bank the experience they are gaining with the ultimate plan of starting their own business a few years into the future.

I can truly say that the tour business is not "rocket science", nor is it "brain surgery". It is an endeavor that anyone with some business sense, a love for the adventure of travel and a sincere interest in building long-term relationships with other human beings, can throw themselves into and come out a winner.

It would be great to hear from any of you who have read this book and who have found the courage to start your own tour business. Feel free to comment or ask questions about what I have written. Actual on-site consulting can be possible at a negotiated rate plus travel expenses.

Please don't call the number (928 680-4142) shown on some of the figures in the Illustrations Section, which will take you, not to me, but to the new owners of Bartlett Tours.

I would prefer emails, but either way, I will be glad to talk with you about this book or about your plans to start a profitable tour business.

My email address is gbartlet@citlink.net

My phone number is 928 846-4101 or cell phone 928 210-6613.

Whatever you do with the rest of your life, remember,

"It's the experience"!

Illustrations

Figure 1 - Home Page of the 2007 Bartlett Tours website.

(Scroll down for all four pages)

Note: When we sold our tour business in 2012, I didn't think to save a digital copy of our last website. When I did need it for this book it was too late. My webmaster found a 2007 version, and thus, it is shown above.

A screenshot of the "About Us" page on our website

4065 Northstar Drive Lake Havasu City Arizona 86406
(928) 680-4142

Serving Lake Havasu since 1993

"It's the Experience."	Home	About Us	Tours	FAQs	Contact Us	Insurance

TOURS:

Branson in the Spring Time

Durango, Silverton & Southwest Colorado

Utah Canyon Country

Thanksgiving California Coast & Baja Cruise

Christmas Musical Shows Tour

Reagan Library & More

San Francisco & The Napa Wine Country

Tahiti & The French Polynesian Islands

Gordon and Patty Bartlett

"It's the experience"

We use our travel experience to make yours memorable

When you travel, it's not just the destination that's important. It's not just the route or the scenery or the people you meet along the way that are important. Rather, I think you'll agree, it's the total experience of the travel that is the important thing. That's why two years ago we adopted the motto, "It's the experience."

We feel the motto also refers to the experience we now have in planning and conducting tours. Bartlett Tours is in it's 15th year offering quality tours to Lake Havasu travelers.

As of April 2007 we have conducted 121 tours with a total passenger count of 5,024 people. Of those 121 tours, 24 have been ocean or river cruises and 23 have involved travel outside the United States. We have a high number of repeat travelers - nearly 600 have taken two or more tours, over 200 have taken 5 or more, and over 60 have taken 10 or more tours. On every 5th tour, our guest receive a "Frequent Traveler" certificate good for dinner at Shugrue's, Barley Brothers or Javelina Cantina in Lake Havasu City. As of April 2007 we have given out 430 dinner certificates to show our appreciation to those who are repeat travelers.

190

A screenshot of the "Tours" page from our website. By scrolling down, our customers would be able to see all our tours.

4065 Northstar Drive Lake Havasu City Arizona 86406
(928) 680-4142

Serving Lake Havasu since 1993

| *"It's the Experience."* | Home | About Us | Tours | FAQs | Contact Us | Insurance |

Tours Scheduled For 2007 - 2008

Schedule updated April 16, 2007

May 7-15, 2007 (9 days)

BRANSON IN THE SPRINGTIME

$1,775

Enjoy springtime in Branson with time to explore the Ozarks. We'll bus to Las Vegas, fly to Kansas City, then travel to Precious Moments in Carthage, MO to overnight. The next morning we'll tour the world-renowned Precious Moments Chapel and Center then travel on to Branson in time for dinner and an evening show. We will see 11 of the best shows in Branson plus luxury accommodations at the Radisson. Planned shows include the hot ones - Daniel O'Donnell, Shoji Tabuchi and Yakov Smirnoff, plus other new and exciting shows. We'll explore the Ozarks at Dogwood Canyon with a special tour and box lunch, plus a cruise, dinner and show aboard the Showboat Branson Belle on Table Rock Lake. This will be an exciting and fun-packed tour. Call now!

Included: All transportation from LHC including air, admission to all shows and attractions, 7 breakfasts, 4 lunches, 8 dinners.

Request space on this tour

191

A screenshot of our "FAQ" (Frequently Asked Questions) page.

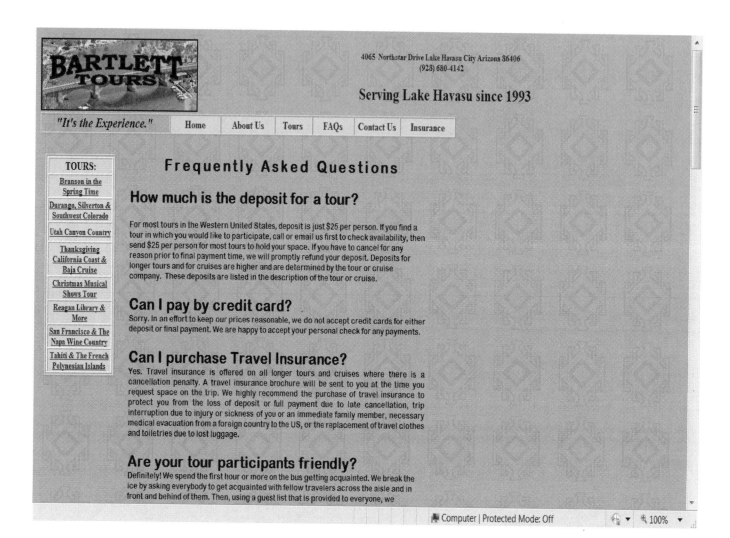

4065 Northstar Drive Lake Havasu City Arizona 86406
(928) 680-4142

Serving Lake Havasu since 1993

"It's the Experience." | Home | About Us | Tours | FAQs | Contact Us | Insurance |

TOURS:

Branson in the Spring Time

Durango, Silverton & Southwest Colorado

Utah Canyon Country

Thanksgiving California Coast & Baja Cruise

Christmas Musical Shows Tour

Reagan Library & More

San Francisco & The Napa Wine Country

Tahiti & The French Polynesian Islands

Frequently Asked Questions

How much is the deposit for a tour?

For most tours in the Western United States, deposit is just $25 per person. If you find a tour in which you would like to participate, call or email us first to check availability, then send $25 per person for most tours to hold your space. If you have to cancel for any reason prior to final payment time, we will promptly refund your deposit. Deposits for longer tours and for cruises are higher and are determined by the tour or cruise company. These deposits are listed in the description of the tour or cruise.

Can I pay by credit card?

Sorry. In an effort to keep our prices reasonable, we do not accept credit cards for either deposit or final payment. We are happy to accept your personal check for any payments.

Can I purchase Travel Insurance?

Yes. Travel insurance is offered on all longer tours and cruises where there is a cancellation penalty. A travel insurance brochure will be sent to you at the time you request space on the trip. We highly recommend the purchase of travel insurance to protect you from the loss of deposit or full payment due to late cancellation, trip interruption due to injury or sickness of you or an immediate family member, necessary medical evacuation from a foreign country to the US, or the replacement of travel clothes and toiletries due to lost luggage.

Are your tour participants friendly?

Definitely! We spend the first hour or more on the bus getting acquainted. We break the ice by asking everybody to get acquainted with fellow travelers across the aisle and in front and behind of them. Then, using a guest list that is provided to everyone, we

Computer | Protected Mode: Off   100%

Figure 2 - Screenshot of Streets & Trips overview map with routing to the left.

Death Valley Tour, March 2012.

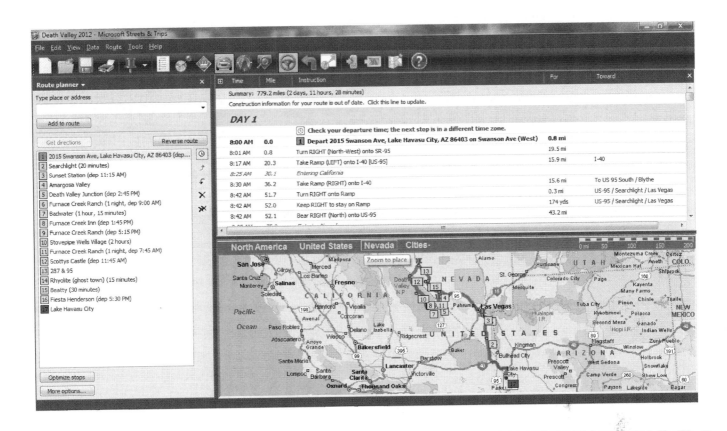

Figure 3 - Detailed Day 1 routing of Death Valley tour from Streets & Trips.

DAY 1

Time	Mile	Instruction	For	Toward
		Check your departure time; the next stop is in a different time zone.		
8:00 AM	**0.0**	**Depart 2015 Swanson Ave, Lake Havasu City, AZ 86403 on Swanson Ave (West)**	**0.8 mi**	
8:01 AM	0.8	Turn RIGHT (North-West) onto SR-95	19.5 mi	
8:17 AM	20.3	Take Ramp (LEFT) onto I-40 [US-95]	15.9 mi	I-40
8:25 AM	*30.1*	*Entering California*		
8:30 AM	36.2	Take Ramp (RIGHT) onto I-40	15.6 mi	To US 95 South / Blythe
8:42 AM	51.7	Turn RIGHT onto Ramp	0.3 mi	US-95 / Searchlight / Las Vegas
8:42 AM	52.0	Keep RIGHT to stay on Ramp	174 yds	US-95 / Searchlight / Las Vegas
8:42 AM	52.1	Bear RIGHT (North) onto US-95	43.2 mi	
9:00 AM	*75.0*	*Entering Nevada*		
9:16 AM	95.3	Turn RIGHT (East) onto (W) Hobson St	0.4 mi	
		Check local time; this stop is in a different time zone.		
9:18 AM	95.7	Turn RIGHT (South) onto Local road(s)	142 yds	
9:18 AM	**95.7**	**Arrive Searchlight**		
9:38 AM	**95.7**	**Depart Searchlight on Local road(s) (North)**	**142 yds**	
9:38 AM	95.8	Turn LEFT (West) onto (E) Hobson St	0.4 mi	
9:40 AM	96.2	Turn RIGHT (North) onto US-95 [S US-93]	36.2 mi	
10:14 AM	132.3	Take Ramp (LEFT) onto US-93 [US-95]	2.8 mi	US-93 / US-95 / Henderson / Las Vegas
10:17 AM	135.1	At exit 56A, take Ramp (LEFT) onto I-515 [US-93]	1.7 mi	Wagonwheel Dr / Nevada State Dr
10:18 AM	136.8	At exit 57, turn off onto Ramp	0.4 mi	College Drive
10:18 AM	137.2	Keep STRAIGHT to stay on Ramp	65 yds	
10:18 AM	137.2	Keep STRAIGHT onto Local road(s)	10 yds	
10:18 AM	137.2	Take Ramp onto I-515 [US-93]	5.8 mi	I-515 / US-93 / US-95
10:23 AM	143.1	At exit 64, turn RIGHT onto Ramp	0.3 mi	Sunset Road
10:23 AM	143.4	Keep LEFT to stay on Ramp	43 yds	I-515
10:23 AM	143.4	Keep STRAIGHT onto Local road(s)	21 yds	
10:23 AM	143.4	Turn LEFT (West) onto SR-562 [W Sunset Rd]	0.6 mi	
10:24 AM	144.0	Turn LEFT (South) onto Galleria Mall	21 yds	
10:25 AM	144.0	Road name changes to Sunset Station Dr	87 yds	
10:25 AM	**144.0**	**Arrive Sunset Station [1301 W Sunset Rd, Henderson NV 89014, United States, Tel: +1 (702) 547-7777]**		
11:15 AM	**144.0**	**Depart Sunset Station [1301 W Sunset Rd, Henderson NV 89014, United States, Tel: +1 (702) 547-7777] on Sunset Station Dr (North)**	**76 yds**	
11:15 AM	144.1	Turn RIGHT (East) onto SR-562 [W Sunset Rd]	0.6 mi	
11:16 AM	144.6	Turn LEFT (North) onto Local road(s)	21 yds	
11:16 AM	144.6	Take Ramp onto I-515 [US-93]	12.2 mi	I-515
11:26 AM	156.9	Road name changes to US-95 [Las Vegas Expy]	0.6 mi	
11:27 AM	157.5	At exit 77, keep RIGHT onto Ramp	0.3 mi	Rancho Drive / US-95-Br
11:27 AM	157.9	Keep RIGHT to stay on Ramp	142 yds	US-95-Br / Rancho Drive
11:27 AM	158.0	Keep STRAIGHT onto US-95 Bus [SR-599]	6.5 mi	
11:34 AM	164.5	Keep STRAIGHT onto Ramp	0.8 mi	US-95
11:35 AM	165.3	Take Ramp (LEFT) onto US-95	2.8 mi	US 95 S
11:37 AM	168.0	At exit 93, take Ramp (RIGHT) onto US-95	73.0 mi	Durango Drive
12:35 PM	241.1	Turn LEFT (South) onto SR-373	142 yds	
12:35 PM	**241.1**	**At Amargosa Valley, stay on SR-373 (South)**	**16.3 mi**	
12:48 PM	*257.5*	*Entering California*		
12:48 PM	257.5	Road name changes to SR-127	7.4 mi	
12:55 PM	264.9	Turn LEFT (East) onto Local road(s)	0.1 mi	
12:56 PM	265.0	Turn LEFT (East) onto Local road(s)	0.1 mi	
12:56 PM	**265.2**	**Arrive Death Valley Junction**		
2:45 PM	**265.2**	**Depart Death Valley Junction on Local road(s)**	**0.1 mi**	
2:45 PM	265.3	Turn RIGHT (North) onto Local road(s)	0.1 mi	
2:45 PM	265.5	Turn RIGHT (North) onto SR-127	0.3 mi	
2:46 PM	265.7	Turn LEFT (West) onto SR-190	29.7 mi	
3:10 PM	295.4	Turn LEFT (West) onto Corral Rd	0.5 mi	

194

Figure 4 - A less detailed itinerary for the driver and myself, as escort.

BARTLETT TOURS
4065 Northstar Drive
Lake Havasu City, AZ 86406

"DEATH VALLEY" - 2012 *ITINERARY*

Monday, March 5, 2012

Deadhead Las Vegas to Lake Havasu City.
Overnight reservations at Lake Place Inn. See Driver directions at end of itinerary.

Tuesday, March 6, 2012
Ar   Lv

7:15		Spot Bus	
		Fenced parking lot behind Lake Place Inn on Swanson.	
	8:00	Departure	
8:00	9:45	North on AZ 95 to I-40 West to Cal95 North to Searchlight,NV	95mi
9:45	10:05	Rest Stop at Terrible's - Searchlight, NV	
		Change to NV time (one hour earlier)	
9:05	10:00	Continue North on 95 into Las Vegas to Sunset Exit, Sunset Station	59mi
10:00	11:15	Lunch at Sunset Station (included)	
11:15	1:15	North on 95 to Amargosa Valley, NV, left on 373 to DV Junction	114mi
1:15	1:30	Restroom break at Amargosa Hotel - 760 852-4441	
1:30	2:45	Tour of Amargosa Opera House & Hotel - Rich	
2:45	3:30	Back 1 block to 190 West to Furnace Creek Ranch	31mi
3:30	4:00	Check in and unload baggage	
4:00	6:00	Free Time	
6:00	7:30	Dinner at the Wrangler Steakhouse	

NO FURTHER USE OF BUS TODAY   299mi

FURNACE CREEK RANCH   **760 786-2345**

195

Wednesday, March 7

		Breakfast at 49'er Cafe or buffet - on your own	
	9:00	Valley Tour - Step-on-guide - Phil Olson	34mi
12:15	1:45	Lunch at Furnace Creek Inn	
1:45	1:50	Travel to Visitor's Center	1mi
1:50	2:45	Free time at Visitor's Center	
2:45	2:50	Travel back to Furnace Creek Ranch - drop at Borax Museum & rooms	1mi
		Borax Museum open 9-9	
3:00	5:15	Free Time	
5:15	6:00	Travel to Stove Pipe Wells for dinner (Sunset 5:50pm)	25mi
6:00	7:50	Dinner at Stove Pipe Wells	
8:00	8:45	Return to Furnace Creek Ranch Show DV Days Video	25mi

NO FURTHER USE OF BUS TODAY   86mi

Thursday, March 8

6:00	7:30	Breakfast at Wrangler Buffet (included)	
		Bags out at 6:30am	
7:45	9:00	Travel North to Scotty's Castle	54mi
9:00	11:45	Scotty's Castle Tour (50 min), Free Time and Lunch	
		Tours in 3 groups - 9:20, 9:30 and 9:40 (19 persons per tour max)	
11:45	1:00	Left out of Scotty's Castle 27 miles to Hwy 95 South	66mi
		through Beatty, bear right on 374 to Rhyolite ghost town (4 miles)	
1:00	1:10	Rhyolite Driving Tour and 1 stop at Bank Building	1mi
1:10	1:20	Travel back to Beatty, left to DV Candy & Nut Co for Rest Stop	5mi
1:20	2:00	Rest Stop in Beatty	
2:00	4:00	South on 95 through Las Vegas to Fiesta Henderson	128mi
		Use Lake Mead exit	
4:00	5:15	Buffet Dinner at Fiesta Henderson	
5:15	6:00	South on 95 to Terrible's in Searchlight	
6:00	6:10	Short Rest Stop	
6:10	7:45	South on 95 to I-40 East to Exit 9 to Lake Havasu City	142mi
		Change to AZ time (one hour later)	
8:45		Back in LHC	

RELEASE BUS   396mi

TOTAL MILES   781mi

DRIVER:

Coming into Lake Havasu City from the north on AZ 95, turn left on Swanson Ave (first signal past the highway overpass). Continue on Swanson until you see a sign "LAKE PLACE INN" on your left. The sign is in the fenced parking lot of the motel. Turn left into the alley (Wings Loop) just before the fenced lot. Follow the alley right just past the motel and go into the office for your room key and the key to the fenced lot. The office is open 24 hours. The motel phone number is 928 855-xxxx.

Please park the bus inside the fenced lot where we will board. Back the bus parellel to the street into the end opposite the alley with the bus centered between the TWO AMBER REFLECTORS on the fence (you will be able to see the amber reflectors in your mirrors). Keep the rear of the bus about 8 feet from the fence. We'll load from that position in the morning.

Please call us when you are at the motel so we can sleep well knowing you're in town.
Call us at 928 680-xxxx. Leave a message if we're not there.

While on tour, Gordon's cell phone is 928 210-xxxx.

Thanks,

Gordon & Patty Bartlett

Figure 5 – Federal Government Per Diem Chart.

Meals and Incidental Expenses (M&IE) Breakdown

The following table is provided for federal employees who need to deduct provided meals from their daily meals and incidental expense (M&IE) allowance. Refer to <u>Section 301-11.18 of the Federal Travel Regulation</u> for specific guidance on deducting these amounts from your per diem reimbursement claims for meals furnished to you by the government. Other organizations may have different rules that apply for their employees; please check with your organization for more assistance.

The table lists the six M&IE tiers in the lower 48 continental United States (currently ranging from $46 to $71). If you need to deduct a meal amount, first determine the location where you will be working while on official travel. You can look up the location-specific information at <u>www.gsa.gov/perdiem</u>. The M&IE rate for your location will be one of the six tiers listed on this table. Find the corresponding amount on the first line of the table (M&IE Total) and then look below for each specific meal deduction amount.

The table also lists the portion of the M&IE rate that is provided for incidental expenses (currently $5 for all tiers), as well as the amount federal employees receive for the first and last calendar day or travel. The first and last calendar day of travel is calculated at 75 percent.

M&IE Total	$46	$51	$56	$61	$66	$71
Continental Breakfast/ Breakfast	$7	$8	$9	$10	$11	$12
Lunch	$11	$12	$13	$15	$16	$18
Dinner	$23	$26	$29	$31	$34	$36
Incidentals	$5	$5	$5	$5	$5	$5
First & Last Day of Travel	$34.50	$38.25	$42	$45.75	$49.50	$53.25

Figure 6 – Expense form for recording expenses while scouting or escorting.

BARTLETT TOURS, INC - Expense Report

| Reason for Trip | Scouting | **Report Period** | From: | 07/25/2011 | **Tour:** | Yosemite |
| | | | To: | 07/29/2011 | | |

Date	7/25	7/26	7/27	7/28	7/29	
End of Day Point	**Mammoth Mtn**	**Mammoth Mtn**	**Portal**	**Tehachapi**	**Lake Havasu**	**TOTALS**
Employee Paid Expenses						
Parking/Tolls						0.00
Meals (per diem)	61.00	61.00	71.00	46.00	46.00	285.00
Admissions						0.00
Porterage	5.00					5.00
Miscellaneous						0.00
Daily Totals	66.00	61.00	71.00	46.00	46.00	290.00
Company Paid Expenses						
Airfare						0.00
Car Rental	181.35				96.16	277.51
Lodging	89.27	89.27	159.84	82.68		421.06
Miscellaneous						0.00
Daily Totals	**270.62**	**89.27**	**159.84**	**82.68**	**96.16**	**698.57**

	Total Expenses:	988.57
	Less: Company Paid	698.57
Employee Signature: _____		
	Due Employee:	290.00
Date: _____		

Figure 7 – Profit Projection for a tour to Death Valley, California.

BARTLETT TOURS - DEATH VALLEY TOUR 2012

MARCH 6-8, 2012	PER PERSON 47	TOTAL 47	SINGLE
DAY 1 - TUE 3/6			
BUS CHARTER - All Aboard America	91.21	4287.00	91.21
DRIVER ROOM LHC	1.05	49.47	1.05
COOKIES & COFFEE	0.64	30.00	0.64
SNACKS ON BOARD	3.00	141.00	3.00
LUNCH AT SUNSET CASINO	11.17	524.99	11.17
TOUR OF AMARGOSA OPERA HOUSE	5.00	235.00	5.00
FURNACE CREEK RANCH LODGING	66.64	3132.08	133.28
LODGING FOR DRIVER	1.31	61.60	1.31
PORTERAGE & MAID TIP (Mandatory)	5.00	235.00	5.00
DINNER – WRANGLER STEAK HOUSE	40.00	1880.00	40.00
DRIVER & ESCORTS	2.55	120.00	2.55
NATIONAL PARK ENTRANCE FEE	4.26	200.00	4.26
DAY 2 - WED 3/7			
STEP-ON GUIDE	3.19	150.00	3.19
LUNCH AT FURNACE CREEK INN	25.00	1175.00	25.00
FURNACE CREEK RANCH LODGING	66.64	3132.08	133.28
MAID TIP	1.00	47.00	1.00
DRIVERS ROOM	1.31	61.60	1.31
DINNER AT STOVE PIPE WELLS	25.00	1175.00	25.00
DAY 3 THU 3/8			
BREAKFAST AT WRANGLER	14.00	658.00	14.00
BREAKFAST FOR 1 ESCORT	0.30	14.00	0.30
SCOTTY'S CASTLE TOUR	10.00	470.00	10.00
CASTLE FOR ESCS & DRVR	0.64	30.00	0.64
BOX LUNCH FROM F C RANCH	22.00	1034.00	22.00
DINNER AT FIESTA HENDERSON	13.65	641.55	13.65
TIP TO DRIVER	1.28	60.00	1.28
PARKING FOR 3 DAYS	2.13	100.00	2.13
TOTAL COST	417.97	19644.37	551.25
CHARGE PER GUEST	**549.00**	25803.00	682.28
NET PROFIT	131.03	**6158.63**	131.03

Figure 8 - Example of the profit from a tour with 30 travelers. See the next two examples to compare the tour with 40 and then with 48 travelers.

BARTLETT TOURS PALM SPRINGS FOLLIES 2012

FEBRUARY 15-16, 2012	PER PERSON	TOTAL
	30	30
DAY 1 - WED 2/15		
BUS CHARTER	**108.36**	**3250.65**
DRIVER ROOM LHC	1.67	50.00
ROLLS & COFFEE	1.00	30.00
SNACKS ON BOARD	2.00	60.00
LUNCH ON OWN IN PALM SPRINGS	0.00	0.00
PALM MOUNTAIN RESORT @$89+tax	51.40	1542.00
LODGING FOR DRIVER	0.00	0.00
PORTERAGE	4.00	120.00
DINNER AT ROCK GARDEN CAFE	18.00	540.00
DRIVER & ESCORTS	1.80	54.00
PALM SPRINGS FOLLIES	49.00	1470.00
FOLLIES FOR DRVR/ESC	3.27	98.00
DAY 2 THU 2/16		
RUBY'S EGG BREAKFAST	5.00	150.00
PS AIR MUSEUM	12.00	360.00
PARKING	2.50	75.00
TOTAL COST	259.99	7799.65
CHARGE PER GUEST	319.00	9570.00
NET PROFIT	**59.01**	**1770.35**

Figure 9 – Example of the profit from the same tour with 40 travelers.

BARTLETT TOURS PALM SPRINGS FOLLIES 2012

FEBRUARY 15-16, 2012	PER PERSON	TOTAL
	40	40
DAY 1 - WED 2/15		
BUS CHARTER	**81.27**	**3250.65**
DRIVER ROOM LHC	1.25	50.00
ROLLS & COFFEE	0.75	30.00
SNACKS ON BOARD	2.00	80.00
LUNCH ON OWN IN PALM SPRINGS	0.00	0.00
PALM MOUNTAIN RESORT @$89+tax	51.40	2056.00
LODGING FOR DRIVER	0.00	0.00
PORTERAGE	4.00	160.00
DINNER AT ROCK GARDEN CAFE	18.00	720.00
DRIVER & ESCORTS	1.35	54.00
PALM SPRINGS FOLLIES	49.00	1960.00
FOLLIES FOR DRVR/ESC	2.45	98.00
DAY 2 THU 2/16		
RUBY'S EGG BREAKFAST	5.00	200.00
PS AIR MUSEUM	12.00	480.00
PARKING	1.88	75.00
TOTAL COST	230.34	9213.65
CHARGE PER GUEST	319.00	12760.00
NET PROFIT	**88.66**	**3546.35**

Figure 10 – Example of the profit from the same tour with 48 travelers.

BARTLETT TOURS PALM SPRINGS FOLLIES 2012

FEBRUARY 15-16, 2012	PER PERSON	TOTAL
	48	48
DAY 1 - WED 2/15		
BUS CHARTER	**67.72**	**3250.65**
DRIVER ROOM LHC	1.04	50.00
ROLLS & COFFEE	0.63	30.00
SNACKS ON BOARD	2.00	96.00
LUNCH ON OWN IN PALM SPRINGS	0.00	0.00
PALM MOUNTAIN RESORT @$89+tax	51.40	2467.20
LODGING FOR DRIVER	0.00	0.00
PORTERAGE	4.00	192.00
DINNER AT ROCK GARDEN CAFE	18.00	864.00
DRIVER & ESCORTS	1.13	54.00
PALM SPRINGS FOLLIES	49.00	2352.00
FOLLIES FOR DRVR/ESC	2.04	98.00
DAY 2 THU 2/16		
RUBY'S EGG BREAKFAST	5.00	240.00
PS AIR MUSEUM	12.00	576.00
PARKING	1.56	75.00
TOTAL COST	215.52	10344.85
CHARGE PER GUEST	319.00	15312.00
NET PROFIT	**103.48**	**4967.15**

Figure 11 – Examples of different newspaper "display" ads for the same tour. I always did my own ad layout and copy with Microsoft Publisher before sending it to the newspaper. Note the use of a consistent business logo in all ads except the "article type" ad in Figure 12.

Figure 12 – Example of an "article type" ad featuring more detail about a single tour. Use of a logo in this type ad was not appropriate.

Bartlett Tours offering tour to Utah's Canyon Country

Limited space is still available on an exciting 6-day tour to the beautiful and cool canyon country of southern Utah.

Join a friendly, local group on this October 16-21 bus tour escorted by Gordon and Patty Bartlett. Fenced, locked parking is provided on Swanson Avenue for your car.

The tour will include stops at Monument Valley and Goose Necks State Park, with visits to the spectacular National Parks of Arches, Canyonlands, Capitol Reef, Bryce and Zion. The group will experience a memorable evening sound and light show by boat on the Colorado River near Moab.

The price of the tour is $895 per person, double-occupancy, and includes all transportation, lodging, admissions, and 14 meals. Single price is $1,133.

For reservations, call Bartlett Tours today at 680-4142 or visit www.BartlettTours.com.

Figure 13 – Example of a larger newspaper ad that we ran to call attention to our business and to alert potential travelers to our upcoming tours. Our local newspaper would occasionally offer us a larger ad as "space available" on short notice but at very advantageous rates.

Bartlett Tours still going strong after 17 years in Lake Havasu City

Bartlett Tours recently celebrated 17 years of offering quality escorted group tours and cruises all from Lake Havasu.

Gordon & Patty Bartlett started the company in early 1993, soon after moving to Lake Havasu City. Since that time, the Bartlett's have escorted a total of 153 tours and cruises all over the world, averaging 44 passengers per tour.

Bartlett Tours' remaining 2010 schedule includes the Back Roads of New England in October, Thanksgiving on the Queen Mary in November and a California Christmas Shows tour in early December.

The early 2011 schedule includes a Mexican Riviera cruise, Palm Springs Follies, a new peach blossom tour into California and a tour to Tucson, Tombstone and Kartchner Caverns in March. A new 2011-2012 schedule will be mailed in mid-September. Call today to be on the Bartlett Tours' mailing list or visit www.BartlettTours.com.

680-4142

BARTLETT TOURS

Figure 14 – Our ad in the season program for a local live musical theatre.

Figure 15 – Example of our ad in a community arts brochure.

208

Figure 16 - A copy of one of our tour brochures, mailed 2 times a year.

Tours & Cruises

BARTLETT TOURS

4065 Northstar Drive
Lake Havasu City, AZ 86406

(928) 680-4142

www.BartlettTours.com

**2011 - 2013
Tour Schedule**

With Bartlett Tours,
"It's the experience"

Our 19th Year in Lake Havasu City

Call to be added to our mailing list.

BARTLETT TOURS

Gordon & Patty Bartlett   (928) 680-4142   October 2011

Check your "Bucket List"

Who even knew what a "bucket list" was before the movie starring Jack Nicholson and Morgan Freeman came out in 2007? We found out a "bucket list" is a list of things that a person wants to do or see before they "kick the bucket". Over the past three years I've had several people say they are signing up for one of our tours because its been on their bucket list. Check your bucket list and see if one of our tours or cruises isn't on it. Then, sign up with us and you'll be on the way to scratching that item off your list.

We need your email address

Please send an email to *Gordon@BartlettTours.com* unless you just received an email from us in the last few days.

WHY?? So we can easily notify you if we have a few seats left on an upcoming tour. Maybe your plans have changed and you now are able to join us or possibly you have already signed up but have friends that would like to go. We can promise you this - we won't sell or give away your email address! We won't send but a handful of emails all year and we won't ever announce a new tour only by email. Thanks!

209

2011/2012 TOUR SCHEDULE

October 16-21, 2011 (6 days)   **UTAH CANYON COUNTRY** $895

One of our most spectacular natural treasures is nearby in Southern Utah. We'll visit Monument Valley, Arches and Canyonlands National Parks near Moab, Capitol Reef, Bryce and Zion. There were 4 spaces available at the time this brochure was sent to the printer, so call immediately to see if we have space for you. This is a beautiful tour!

Included: All transportation, lodging, all admissions, step-on-guide, 4 breakfasts, 5 lunches, 5 dinners.

November 21-25, 2011 (5 days)   **THANKSGIVING CALIFORNIA COAST & BAJA CRUISE**   From $769

Don't be alone on Thanksgiving. We escorted a group on this cruise over Thanksgiving 2009 and everyone had a great time! Enjoy a relaxing 4-night cruise aboard the *Carnival Paradise* down the California coast and the Baja California peninsula of Mexico. Our ports-of-call will be Catalina Island, California and Ensenada, Mexico. Inside cabin (no window) $769; outside cabin with window $799; balcony suites at $1,139; all prices per person, double occupancy. This cruise is sold out but call for last-minute availability.

Included: Transportation from LHC, 4-night cruise, luggage handling, 2 lunches en route, all meals and entertainment on board.

December 5-12, 2011 (8 days)   **BRANSON BEFORE CHRISTMAS** $1,995

Branson is a special place, and before Christmas, it's magical! Don't miss this opportunity to see nine of the top shows in Branson, including Japanese violinist Shoji Tabuchi, Andy Williams, Tony Orlando & the Lennon Sisters, the Twelve Irish Tenors and Yakov Smirnoff. In addition to the fabulous entertainment, we'll also tour the area, visit old downtown Branson, have some great meals and view the Branson Festival of Lights. Weather is mild, generally in the mid-50's at this time of year and usually too early for snow. You'll come away from each show uplifted, joyous and in the Christmas spirit! Call for availability.

Included: All air and ground transportation, all admissions, local tour guide, 5 breakfasts and 6 dinners.

January 18-20, 2012 (3 days)   **LAKE MEAD & VALLEY OF FIRE** $419

Be ready for awe-inspiring natural beauty on this tour! We will travel to Boulder City, NV where we'll enjoy lunch at the historic Boulder Dam Hotel, built in 1933 to house engineers and foremen building Boulder Dam (later named Hoover Dam). We'll visit the very interesting Boulder Dam Museum and take a 90-minute narrated cruise on lower Lake Mead with views of Hoover Dam. We'll spend both nights at the Fiesta Henderson Casino. We'll travel by bus up the west and north sides of Lake Mead, through what could be called Nevada's "painted desert" and enjoy a box lunch in the Valley of Fire State Park. Aptly named, the Valley of Fire is full of jagged, bright red peaks and scenic valleys worthy of photos. Returning to Henderson, we'll drive over Hoover Dam and over the new bridge just opened in 2010. On day three, we'll visit the excellent Clark County Heritage Museum. Space is still available.

Included: All transportation, lodging, all admissions, 2 breakfasts, 3 lunches, 2 dinners.

NEW **February 6-9, 2012 (4 days)**   **BRANSONFEST OUT WEST** $479

Branson entertainment has come to Mesquite Nevada! This is the third year that Mesquite has hosted this Branson-style festival with professional impersonators entertaining us while the Branson theaters are closed for the winter. The first evening show, *"Branson is Country"*, will highlight country music and entertainers offering tributes to Johnny Cash, Willie Nelson and other favorites. The second evening show is entitled *"Branson is Variety"* featuring tributes to Elvis, Dean Martin, Tony Bennett and the hilarious comedy of "Harley Worthit". The third evening show, *"Branson is Patriotic"* features Igor and the Jazz Cowboys and an array of other entertainers paying a musical tribute to our great country. During the second and third mornings you can choose from line or country dance lessons, fun and fitness classes or making new friends. Enjoy an afternoon matinee each day featuring senior (over age 60) entertainers. We'll be staying at the Casablanca Resort where all the activities are centered. Reserve now with just $25.

Included: Transportation, lodging, admissions to evening and matinee shows, 3 breakfasts and 3 dinners.

February 15-16, 2012 (2 days)   **PALM SPRINGS FOLLIES** $319

Enjoy excellent main floor seats for the evening performance of the fabulous Palm Springs Follies - a show in the tradition of the Ziegfeld Follies with the joyous dance and music of the 40's, 50's and 60's live again. All the singers, dancers and performers are between the ages of 50 and 80+. Many have been singing and dancing professionally all their lives. The costumes and sets rival anything seen in Las Vegas. Included is a guided tour of the Palm Springs Air Museum which houses the largest collection of WWII flyable aircraft. Most of the guides flew on these same aircraft in World War II and their stories are amazing. We'll stay at the Palm Mountain Resort in downtown Palm Springs, just one block from the Follies. Limited space available. $25 per person to book now.

Included: Transportation, lodging, all admissions, 1 breakfast, 1 dinner.

March 6-8, 2012 (3 days)   **DEATH VALLEY & SCOTTY'S CASTLE** $549

The beauty of the desert in Death Valley National Park is breathtaking! We'll stay two nights at Furnace Creek Ranch right in Death Valley. Within the complex of Furnace Creek Ranch is the U S Borax Museum, with stories and pictures of the borax mines and the famous 20-mule teams. See old mining equipment, a train and an actual wagon pulled by the mule teams. Enjoy a special guided tour of the Lower Valley and lunch at the elegant and historic Furnace Creek Inn built in 1923. We'll see the National Park Visitor's Center and have dinner at the little settlement of Stove Pipe Wells. Our third morning we'll have a guided tour of the fabulous Scotty's Castle, completed in 1931. Just a few spaces left. Don't miss this one. $25 per person deposit.

Included: Luxury transportation, lodging, all tours and admissions, 1 breakfast, 2 lunches, 3 dinners.

928 680-4142

210

2012 TOUR SCHEDULE

April 28-May 5, 2012 (8 days)   PACIFIC COASTAL CRUISE   from $1,195

Sail on the *Sapphire Princess* roundtrip from Los Angeles to our ports-of-call in Santa Barbara, San Francisco, San Diego and Ensenada, Mexico. Shore excursions will offer you the chance to see elegant Santa Barbara and the beautiful Santa Barbara Mission founded by Padre Junipero Serra. After sailing under the Golden Gate Bridge into San Francisco Bay, choose from a city tour, the Alcatraz Federal Penitentiary tour or a tour of the Napa Valley wine country. In San Diego, enjoy the embarcadero where the ship docks, take a city tour, or choose to board the aircraft carrier USS Midway, now a floating museum. The USS Midway is within sight and easy walking distance from our ship. In Ensenada, enjoy one of several tours or take a short shuttle ride into town for some great shopping. We have Inside cabins (no window) at $1,195; Window cabins at $1,435 and Balcony cabins at $1,595. All prices are per person, double occupancy. Single prices $1,675, $2,075 and $2,795 respectively. Join us on this fun and exciting cruise. Deposit is $250 per person and is fully refundable until final payment time, February 6, 2012. Space is still available on this cruise. Call today!

Included: Transportation from LHC, lunch en route each way, luggage handling and all meals and entertainment on board. Shore excursions and onboard gratuities (currently $70 per passenger) are not included in the prices above.

July 16-19, 2012 (4 days)   YOSEMITE NATIONAL PARK $795

Leave the Havasu heat behind for a few days of delightful cool! We will travel to Merced the first day, overnight, then enter the West gate into Yosemite National Park, one of the most picturesque of all national parks. Once in Yosemite Valley (elevation 4,000) we will take a 2-hour Valley Floor tour on a 60-passenger open vehicle where you will have unobstructed views of the water falls and the glacier-carved granite mountains while a National Park Ranger narrates. Immediately after our tour, our charter bus will take us to the historic Ahwahnee Hotel for lunch in the fabulous dining room with huge granite pillars and sugar pine beams. The Ahwahnee Hotel was built in 1927 and the dining room is its "crown jewel". After lunch, there will be time to enjoy the lobby and sitting room of the hotel as well as the outside patios. We'll leave Yosemite Valley for our lodging just outside the West gate where the balcony of each room is just steps away from the untamed Merced River. The next day we will re-enter Yosemite, visit the Pioneer Historic Center and have lunch in the historic Wawona Hotel (1879) before leaving the park for our last night in Bakersfield. $25 to reserve.

Included: Transportation, lodging, all admissions, Valley Floor tour, 3 breakfasts, 3 lunches, 3 dinners.

October 15-29, 2012 (15 days)   AUSTRALIA & NEW ZEALAND $5,375

In response to many requests, we are once again offering a land and air tour of Australia and New Zealand. October is spring "down under", and offers the best weather for travel in these two beautiful countries. We will fly from Los Angeles to Cairns, Australia where we will be met by our Collette Vacations tour manager. The highlights of the tour will be: Cairns – the Aboriginal Cultural Center, a crocodile farm, the Great Barrier Reef; Sydney - the Sydney Opera House, the Harbour Bridge, Chinatown and a dinner cruise in Sydney Harbour; Christchurch, New Zealand - the Neo-Gothic Cathedral, farm visit, dinner at the Riccarton House mansion, and a home-cooked meal in the home of a local family; Mt Cook Region - view glaciers and jagged, snow-covered mountains; Queenstown - a beautiful cruise on Milford Sound, dinner at the Skyline Restaurant. Call for a detailed itinerary. $250 deposit.

Included: All air & ground transportation, lodging, all admissions, Collette Tour Manager, 12 breakfasts, 4 lunches, 6 dinners.

November 19-23, 2012 (5 days)   THANKSGIVING CALIFORNIA COAST & BAJA CRUISE $779, $809 or $1,149

Be with a group of friendly travelers from Lake Havasu and the river area over Thanksgiving. Enjoy a relaxing 4-night cruise aboard the *Carnival Inspiration* down the California coast and the Baja California peninsula of Mexico. Our ports-of-call will be Catalina Island, California and Ensenada, Mexico. Is Ensenada safe? Yes, we believe as long as you are on a shore excursion or stay on the main shopping street, you will have no problem. Ensenada is not on a drug route nor is it a border town. Use common sense as you would if you were visiting Chicago or Los Angeles and you will enjoy this port city. You'll have a full day in each port to enjoy guided shore excursions and shop on your own. Enjoy great food and exciting evening entertainment on board our ship. Leaving Monday morning, we'll be back in LHC Friday afternoon. Inside cabin (no window) $779; outside cabin with window, $809; balcony suites at $1,149; all prices per person, double occupancy. Due to a new Carnival policy, early or late dining can only be chosen at time of reservation and deposit. Early dining cannot be assured unless you make your reservation early. Reserve now with just $150 per person deposit which is fully refundable up until final payment date of September 13, 2012. Don't miss this!

Included: Transportation from LHC, 4-night cruise, luggage handling, 2 lunches en route, all meals and entertainment on board.

December 14-16, 2012 (3 days)   SOUTHERN CALIFORNIA CHRISTMAS SHOWS $495

Get into the Christmas spirit by joining us on this exciting Christmas musicals tour. The first day we will travel to Ontario and check into the Hampton Inn at Ontario Mills Mall. There will be time for shopping before we leave for a fast-paced song and dance show at Tibbie's in their new theatre in Fontana. The next day we'll have a leisurely morning, then lunch on the way to a matinee at Citrus College where students put on a show with an orchestra, chorus and dancers. This is a very popular show that has been presented at Citrus College for years. After a short rest back at our hotel, we'll head to Riverside and visit the Mission Inn, a National Heritage Landmark. The Inn is decorated for Christmas with over 3 1/2 million lights and over 350 animated figures and you will have time to stroll around and through the Inn to marvel at the decorations. From Riverside, we'll go to the Candlelight Pavilion in Claremont for their evening Christmas dinner show. The third morning we'll depart Ontario and return to Lake Havasu City. Reserve with just $25.

Included: Transportation, lodging, three Christmas shows, 2 breakfasts, 3 lunches, 2 dinners.

www.BartlettTours.com

2013 TOUR SCHEDULE

January 6-13, 2013 (8 days)   MEXICAN RIVIERA CRUISE $919, $999 or $1,159

This is a great way to see Mexico without worrying about the food and water. You sleep in the same stateroom each night and enjoy the great food onboard the beautiful *Carnival Splendor*. The west coast of Mexico is far from the route for those bringing drugs to the US. In our opinion, visiting Mexican ports-of-call is safer than visiting many large US cities, especially Washington, DC. The international staff will work hard to make this an enjoyable cruise for you. Each night you will experience great dinners and fabulous broadway-style entertainment. During the day, enjoy the many activities on board our ship. Shore excursions are available in our two ports-of-call, Cabo San Lucas (two days) and Puerto Vallarta. The weather is generally in the low to mid-80's at this time of year. We provide motorcoach transportation from Lake Havasu City to the ship and arrange for the handling of your luggage so you can relax and have fun. Select from inside cabins (no window) at $919; oceanview cabins at $999 and balcony cabins at $1,159. Prices are per person based on double occupancy. Single occupancy prices are $1,378, $1,538 and $$1,858 respectively. A valid passport is required. The deposit is $250 per person at booking. Call or email us for a detailed itinerary.

Included: LHC to pier and return, 2 Sunday dinners en route, luggage handling, 7-night cruise with all meals and entertainment.

February 18-21, 2013 (4 days)   SAN DIEGO SAMPLER TOUR $775

Join us for an exciting tour to San Diego. Upon arrival, we'll have a sunset harbor cruise and view the beautiful city from the water. We'll have a guided tour of San Diego and learn about its rich heritage. An afternoon will be spent at the world-class San Diego Zoo, first with a narrated tram ride and then with time to visit your favorite exhibits on your own. We will visit Balboa Park, the site of the Panama-California exposition in 1915-16 in celebration of the opening of the Panama Canal. Here you will have a choice of up to four museums to visit including the Museum of San Diego History, the Reuben H Fleet Science Center, the Botanical Building, the Museum of Photographic Arts, the San Diego Air & Space Museum, the Hall of Champions Sports Museum, the Automotive Museum or the San Diego Museum of Art. A free tram runs every 10 minutes so you can visit <u>four museums</u>. Later, you will have time on your own to visit the historic Star of India sailing vessel, the Maritime Museum or, for the fittest among us, the USS Midway, a WWII aircraft carrier. We'll also enjoy some great dinners along the waterfront and in the Gas Lamp district of San Diego. All three nights in the Bay Club Hotel on Shelter Island. Choose to join us on this exciting tour. Reserve now with just $25.

Included: All transportation, lodging, admissions, 3 breakfasts, 2 lunches, 3 dinners.

March 18-23, 2013 (6 days)   CALIFORNIA COAST & HEARST CASTLE $975

This is one of our most popular tours. We travel by motorcoach to Ventura where we stay at the Crowne Plaza. Our hotel is right on the beach with a boardwalk and the Ventura Pier nearby. Next morning we'll visit the Santa Barbara Mission, then have lunch and free time in Solvang, a unique Danish village. Next day we'll visit the fabulous Hearst Castle where we'll see the National Geographic film on the building of the castle, then have a guided tour of the 57-bedroom "ranch house" of William Randolph Hearst. Then its on to Monterey for two nights. We'll have dinner on famous "Cannery Row", tour Carmel and the 17-mile Drive, stroll Monterey's Old Fisherman's Wharf, and visit the world famous Monterey Bay Aquarium. On our way home, we'll travel through the San Joaquin Valley to Bakersfield, overnight, then travel back to LHC. This is a great scenic tour! Reserve now with just $25.

Included: All transportation, lodging, all admissions, 3 breakfasts, 2 lunches, 5 dinners.

Free parking in a fenced and locked lot on Swanson Avenue next to the Lake Place Inn.
All prices shown are per person based on double occupancy. Single room prices are higher.
Itineraries described in this schedule are subject to change or cancellation.
Prices shown in this schedule are subject to change.
Fuel surcharges may be imposed by airlines and cruise lines and, if any, will be due at time of final billing.

$25 Deposit On Most Tours

If you find a tour in which you would like to participate, call first, then send just $25 per person for most tours to hold your space. If you have to cancel for any reason, we will promptly refund your money. Major tour and cruise deposits are higher.

All Tours Are Fully Escorted

Gordon and Patty Bartlett escort all tours and cruises to make your travel experience as full and easy as possible. All of our tours and cruises leave from Lake Havasu City, so you don't need to drive to an airport in Las Vegas or Phoenix to begin your tour. When you travel with Bartlett Tours, you are also freed from luggage handling at airports and hotels on all tours longer than 2 days. It's more fun to travel with Bartlett Tours!

Responsibility

Bartlett Tours, Inc., acts only as agent on behalf of bus operators, airlines, railroads, cruise lines, restaurants, hotels and motels, attractions, tour operators and sightseeing providers subcontracted and shall in no instance be liable for any injury, loss or other shortcomings resulting from the performance of those principals, their employees or agents. You will receive our complete Terms and Conditions with your first tour confirmation or upon request.

Pricing Of Our Tours

All prices shown are per person based on double occupancy. Singles are welcome, but single room prices are higher. Prices and itineraries shown in this schedule are subject to change.

928 680-4142   **Email: Gordon@BartlettTours.com**

Figure 17 – Sample Confirmation Letter sent to guests 45-60 days ahead of tour.

BARTLETT TOURS, Inc.
4065 Northstar Drive
Lake Havasu City, AZ 86406
928 680-xxxx

January 16, 2012

Dear _____:

Thank you for your reservation for our March 6-8, 2012 **"Death Valley & Scotty's Castle"** tour. The price of the tour is $549 (single room is $680).

This will confirm that we have received your deposit of $_____ and are holding _____ space(s) for you. Please use the enclosed envelope to send us the balance of $_____ by **February 3rd**.

We will depart at 8:00am SHARP, on Tuesday, March 6 from the parking lot on the Swanson Avenue side of the Lake Place Inn (in the 2000 block of Swanson). The parking lot is fenced and will be locked while we are gone. You may enter the parking lot from Swanson. The gate will be open at 7:25am. You will see the bus parked inside the lot where we will board.

When you arrive you will receive a "boarding pass" numbered in the sequence of your original reservation (not your arrival time at the parking lot). **Plan to arrive between 7:30 & 7:45am** for coffee and cookies before boarding. At 7:50am we will call the boarding passes in sequence and once on board you may select the seats that most appeal to you. This procedure rewards those who made their reservations early.

The itinerary for the trip is on the reverse side of this letter. Casual clothes are appropriate for everything we will be doing on this tour. Be sure to bring good walking shoes. The weather should be mild in Death Valley at this time of year but be sure to bring a sweater or jacket for the evenings.

We will provide bottled water and occasional snacks on the bus for your pleasure and convenience. The bus has a restroom, but we have planned rest stops about every two hours while traveling. One breakfast, two lunches and three dinners are included in the price of the tour.

If this is your first tour with us, please complete the Information Form enclosed and return with your payment.   A copy of our Terms and Conditions is also enclosed.   If you have traveled with us before and your Information Form is over two years old, we have enclosed a new one for you to complete and return.

Thank you very much for choosing to join us. Come with a cheerful attitude, ready to laugh and have fun. This is a great tour! We'll all have a good time!

Sincerely,

Gordon R Bartlett

Figure 18 – Sample of a Guest Itinerary usually printed on the back of the Confirmation Letter.

DEATH VALLEY & SCOTTY'S CASTLE

2012 TOUR ITINERARY

Tuesday, March 6

8:00	Leave LHC
	Rest Stop at Searchlight
	Change to Nevada/California time (one hour earlier)
10:00	Buffet breakfast at Sunset Station (included)
	Visit to Amargosa Opera House
3:30	Furnace Creek Ranch - Check-in and free time
6:00	Dinner at the Wrangler Steakhouse (included)

Wednesday, March 7

	Breakfast on your own in the cafe
9:00	Valley Tour - Guided by Phil Olson
12:00	Tour & Lunch at historic Furnace Creek Inn (included)
	Visit to Death Valley NP Visitor's Center
	Free time at US Borax Museum & Furnace Creek Ranch
5:15	Leave for Stove Pipe Wells
6:00	Dinner at Stove Pipe Wells (included)
8:30	Back at Furnace Creek Ranch

Thursday, March 8

6:00 7:30	Breakfast Buffet at Furnace Creek Ranch (included)
7:45	Leave for Scotty's Castle
9:00	Scotty's Castle - Guided Tour in 3 groups (9:20, 9:30, 9:40)
	Lunch at Scotty's Castle (on your own)
	Driving tour of Rhyolite Ghost Town
4:00	Buffet Dinner at Fiesta Henderson (included)
	Change back to Arizona time (one hour later)
8:45	Back in LHC (Arizona time)

Emergency Numbers:

Furnace Creek Ranch	**760 786-2345**
Gordon's Cell Phone	**928 210-xxxx**

Figure 19 – Information Form sent to travelers on their first tour.

INFORMATION FORM

Please provide the following information so that we can be aware of your needs and make your tour with us as enjoyable as possible. The health information is requested to enable us to get you medical assistance as quickly as possible in case of an emergency while on our tour. The health information requested on this form is purely optional at your discretion. If you choose not to provide the information, please indicate and sign below. In either case, be sure you have your insurance card readily available in your purse or wallet. PLEASE PRINT.

Name _____ Phone _____

Address _____ City _____ State _____ ZIP _____

Preferred First Name for Badge _____ Email Address _____

Date of Birth _____ Do you require a Smoking Room? _____

List any serious physical disabilities or limitations _____

_____

If necessary, are you able to walk up one or two flights of stairs to your room? _____

List any medications you are allergic to _____

_____

Current Medications (with dosages) _____

_____

_____

Your Doctor's Name _____ Phone _____

Primary Insurance Carrier _____ Policy # _____

Name of Person to be Contacted in Case of an Emergency:

Name _____ Relationship _____

Home Phone _____ Work Phone _____

In the event of an emergency, I hereby give my permission to tour escorts of Bartlett Tours accompanying me to secure proper medical care for me as deemed necessary at the time. I hereby release Bartlett Tours from any and all costs and liabilities incurred as a result of said medical care.

I have received a copy of Bartlett Tours' *Terms and Conditions* and understand how they pertain to my participation in any part of this or future tour programs.

❑ I have chosen *NOT* to provide the health information requested above, but will have my insurance identification card with me.

Signature _____ Date _____

BARTLETT TOURS

Figure 20 – Bartlett Tours Terms and Conditions sent with _first_ tour confirmation.

TERMS AND CONDITIONS

The tours offered by Bartlett Tours are designed for the active mature adult. The nature of the overnight tours often requires moderate walking each day, as well as adherence to a schedule.

These tours are operated by Bartlett Tours, Inc. of Lake Havasu City, Arizona. All transportation, sight-seeing excursions, attractions, restaurants, hotel accommodations or other travel services are furnished by them only as agent for the contractors providing the services. Bartlett Tours shall not be held liable for loss of or damage of property, or injury to person, resulting from the performance of those contractors, their employees or servants. By utilizing the services of the suppliers, you agree that your remedy is directly with the suppliers and not with Bartlett Tours.

These tour programs are planned in advance. If, between planning time and the actual tour operation, circumstances beyond our control require changes, we reserve the right to vary itineraries and/or substitute components of our tour programs.

Bartlett Tours reserves the right at any time to dismiss anyone from the tour whose conduct has become injurious to the welfare and pleasure of other tour participants. The dismissed person must make their own arrangements for return home at their expense. No tour refund will be made.

If you choose to leave a vehicle at the departure point, you do so at your own risk. Neither Bartlett Tours nor the owner of the parking lot will be responsible for any loss or damage to your vehicle.

Full and final payment for a reservation on a tour, and/or your participation in any part of a tour, constitutes consent to all provisions of these Terms and Conditions.

BAGGAGE: Each passenger is allowed 1 suitcase (on overnight trips) and a small carry-on bag. On cruises, each person will be allowed up to 2 suitcases plus a small carry-on bag.

CANCELLATION POLICY: There is no penalty charge for cancellation 30 days or more prior to departure, regardless of reason. If you cancel within 30 days from departure, and we are able to fill your space, we will refund in full. If you cancel within 30 days and we cannot fill your space, we can only refund unused, refundable air tickets, lodging, meals and attractions where we are not charged. No refunds will be given for "no shows" or for cancellation after a tour begins.

Where Bartlett Tours organizes the tour but contracts for the operation of the tour with a cruise line or another tour company, cancellation charges will be in line with that other company's policies. In those cases, you will be notified of the cancellation charges and will be offered the opportunity to purchase travel insurance protection.

BARTLETT TOURS
4065 Northstar Drive
Lake Havasu City, AZ 86406

216

Figure 21 – Meal Selection form sometimes sent with Confirmation Letter.

Name _____

MEAL SELECTIONS - 2010 Christmas Shows Tour

DINNER - Thursday, Dec 9 - Lyon's English Grill

Princess Prime Rib   **(circle your choice)**
Slow Roasted to Perfection
Chicken Kensington
Breast of Chicken sauteed in a sherry wine sauce with fresh mushrooms
Filet of Sole Almondine
Grilled till golden brown, sprinkled with toasted almonds

DINNER - Friday, Dec 10 - Tibbie's Cabaret Dinner Theatre

Prime Rib of Beef   **(circle your choice)**
Slow Roasted and <u>served Medium</u>
Salmon Beurre Blanc
Baked Salmon filet topped with white dill sauce
Chicken Florentine
Breast of Chicken stuffed with spinach & Swiss cheese with tomato tarragon sauce
Vegetarian Pasta
Penne pasta tossed with freshly sauteed vegetables

PLEASE RETURN THIS SHEET WITH PAYMENT.   Note your selection on your own itinerary.

Figure 22 – Checklist of things that must be done before tour day.

PRE-TOUR CHECKLIST

Guest Name Badges in alpha order
Boarding Passes - **numbered**
Luggage Tags (clipped to boarding passes)
Passenger Lists for guests (to put on seats)
Meal Selection hand-out (if required)
Frequent Traveler Awards for those with 5, 10, 15, 20, 25, etc. tours
Hotel Rooming Lists
Completed Information Forms for each traveler (in case of illness or injury)
Airline Tickets, if applicable
Event Tickets, if required
Seating Chart for Event
Bus Sign for windshield
Escort Notes for en route comments
Pay for Parking lot
Itinerary for the Driver
Blank Cash Expense Form
Trip File with contracts
Other Handouts?
Bartlett Tours brochures
Reservation slips for onboard reservations
Maps
Joke List
Video DVD's - comedy entertainment
Video DVD's - informational and historic for this tour
Audio (music) CD's
Microphone Cover (foam cover to soften your voice)
Insurance Report Forms in case of injury during tour
Driver Tip Suggestion Sheets to be passed around on last leg of tour
Small Envelopes for guests to provide Driver Tips
Camera with charged batteries & charger
Cellular Phone & charger
Flashlight
Our Escort Badges
CASH for tips, unexpected expenses
Order Cookies & Coffee for pre-departure

Make Phone Calls to first-time travelers afternoon before departure
Change Message on Answering Machine

Departure Morning:
Pick up Cookies and Coffee on way to parking lot

Figure 23 – Examples of Name Badge, Luggage Tag and Boarding Pass.

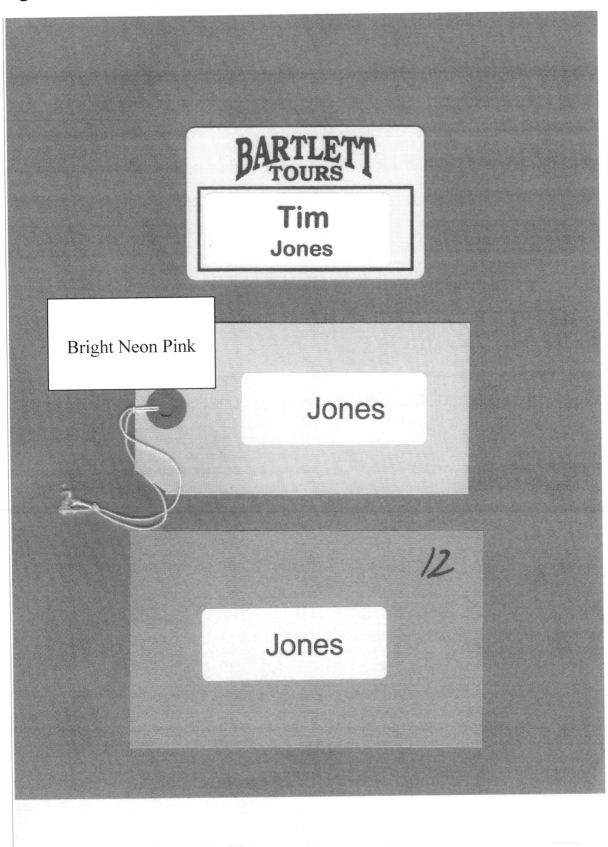

Figure 24 – Example of a page of printed labels for attaching to plastic name badges. (For a look at our badges, see Figure 23)

Bill Brophy	**Tom** Brozic	**John** Byrnes
Jerry Degelbeck	**Henry** Fishburn	**Virg** Goodman
Judy Johnson	**Martha** Knoll	**Angela** Mayson
Lillian Milne	**JoAnn** Minner	**Mike** Mullen
Tom Orr	**Gary** Parenteau	**Dave** Potthoff
Sharron Rhodes	**Cecil** Sisco	**Ernie** Smith
Frank Spielberger	**John** Story	**Mike** Varvis
Edward Willis	**Lora** Winsborough	

Suggest using MACO mailing labels #ML-3000 – self adhesive, 30 labels per sheet.

The customer records system I used required that I print all First Names #1 at one time, then change to those records with a First Name #2 (couples), and print them second.

These labels were then affixed to the white plastic "Bartlett Tours" badges shown earlier.

Figure 25 – Screenshot of last name labels for Luggage Tags and Boarding Passes using "Large3Up" tab to right. (Choosing "3" copies on the printer setup screen will print 3 labels for each name.)

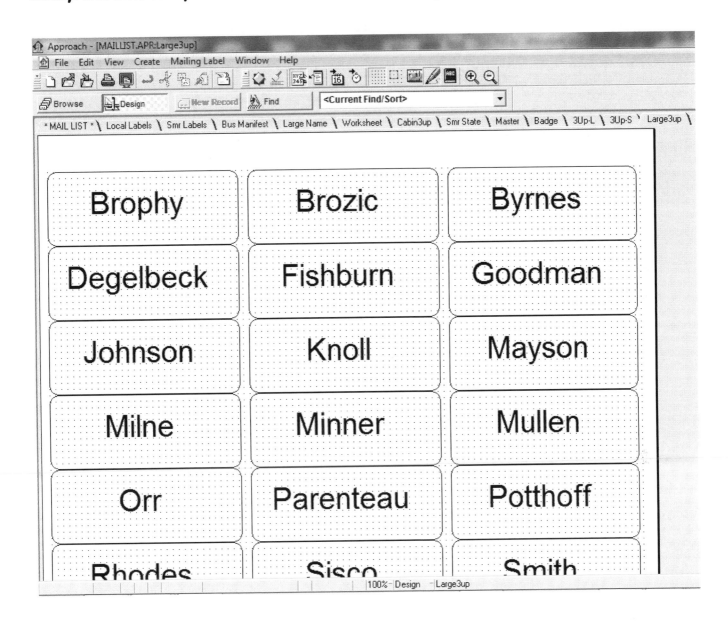

BARTLETT TOURS
Lake Havasu City, Arizona

Death Valley & Scotty's Castle

March 6-8, 2012

ALFERI, Berdene - 4
ALFERI, Cathy - 4
AMOS, Jan - 5
BAIRD, Jerry & Sandy - 2
EMERY, Dale & Barb - 4
GODDARD, Betty - 5
GUSMAN, Frank & Dee - 3
HALL, Joan - 8
HOLLENZER, Ken & Salli - 1
INGALLS, Don & Lois -3
ISAMAN, Lucille - 7
JOHNSON, Judy - 10
KEIPER, Vern & Judy - 4
KENNEDY, Ken & Pat - 5
KERVI, Jack - 1
KIEPE, Lola - 8
LAWRENCE, Char - 2
LEWIS, Shirley - 1
MARIN, Darald & Marlene - 3
McCHESNEY, Al - 4
MOHR, Ron & Mary - 5
MUND, Tom & Shirley - 4
NIXDORF, Jim & Betty - 1
NORELL, Donna - 3
ORR, Tom & Dana - 12
ORTEGO, Buddy & Chris - 5
ROGERS, Phebe - 4
SCHOENBERGER, Ray & Judy - 7
SCOLLARD, Tom & Shirley - 3
VOLLMER, Tami - 2
WESTEDT, Kent & Susan - 9

47

The number beside the name indicates the number of tours with us.

Figure 27 – Picture of the "Spider" hung at the front of the bus to indicate which side will exit first at the next stop. Long nut holds it in the track beneath overhead storage bins. We used bright red yarn.

Figure 28 – Screenshot of the Bus Manifest for the Death Valley tour, 2012

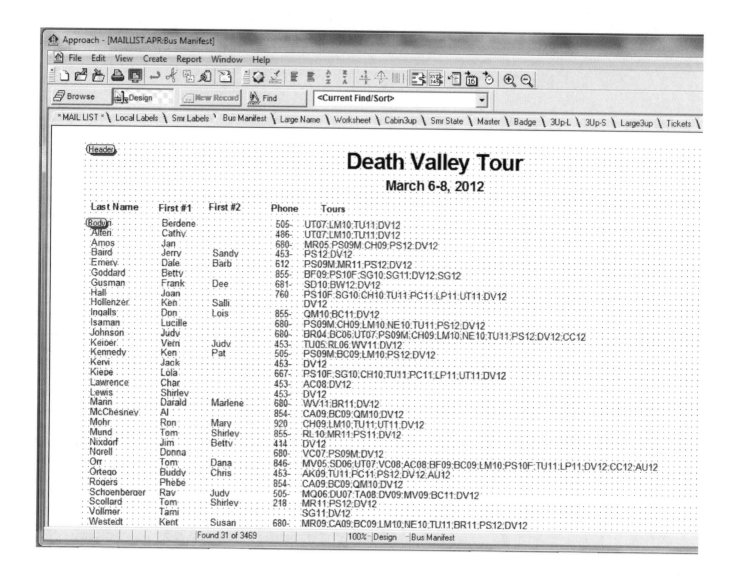

Figure 29 - Tipping Guidelines for our driver at end of the tour.

DRIVER GRATUITY

Our Driver: Wade

It is common practice on motorcoach tours to tip the driver near the end of the trip. The gratuity is not as much for the driving as for the <u>assistance and the baggage handling</u> that the driver does for us during the tour and for keeping the bus clean.

The normal driver tip today is $2.00 - $3.00 per person per day. So, for **each person** on a 3-day tour, $6.00 - $9.00 would be suggested. Of course, you may give more or less, depending on your satisfaction with our driver.

If you would like to place your tip in an envelope, and possibly write a short note, please feel free to take one. Tipping is a personal thing and we suggest that you **hand it to Wade** at our last rest stop prior to arriving back in Lake Havasu.

Gordon & Patty

DRIVER GRATUITY

Our Driver: Wade

It is common practice on motorcoach tours to tip the driver near the end of the trip. The gratuity is not as much for the driving as for the <u>assistance and the baggage handling</u> that the driver does for us during the tour and for keeping the bus clean.

The normal driver tip today is $2.00 - $3.00 per person per day. So, for **each person** on a 3-day tour, $6.00 - $9.00 would be suggested. Of course, you may give more or less, depending on your satisfaction with our driver.

If you would like to place your tip in an envelope, and possibly write a short note, please feel free to take one. Tipping is a personal thing and we suggest that you **hand it to Wade** at our last rest stop prior to arriving back in Lake Havasu.

Gordon & Patty

Figure 30 – Profit Projection of a "Major" tour.

BARTLETT TOURS - PROFIT PROJECTION BACK ROADS OF NEW ENGLAND

NEW ENGLAND - OCT 10-19, 2010

10 DAYS	46 #/PAX	46 TOTAL	SINGLE	TRIPLE	FLY FROM OMAHA	NO AIR TO BOSTON
BUS CHARTER - Ryan's	58.10	2672.76	58.10	58.10		
CREDIT FOR BUS	-50.00	-2300.00	-50.00	-50.00		
BUS DRIVER TIPS (4 TRIPS)	4.35	200.00	4.35	4.35		
ALL SNACKS & WATER	1.09	50.00	1.09	1.09		
OVERNIGHT FIESTA incl dinner	33.17	1393.14	54.04	31.87		
DRIVER OVERNIGHT	1.17	54.04	1.17	1.17		
SKYCAP TIPS LAS (OUT & IN)	3.00	138.00	3.00	3.00		
DINNER IN BOSTON HOTEL	17.39	800.00	17.39	17.39	17.39	17.39
COLLETTE PACKAGE NET	1386.00	63756.00	2086.00	1356.00	1386.00	1386.00
ESCORTS PACKAGE	60.26	2772.00	60.26	60.26	60.26	60.26
COLLETTE AIR LAS VEGAS	540.00	24840.00	540.00	540.00	500.00	0.00
AIR TAXES & SURCHARGE	50.00	2300.00	50.00	50.00	50.00	0.00
ESCORTS AIRFARE & TAX	25.65	1180.00	25.65	25.65	25.65	25.65
OVERNIGHT FIESTA incl bkfst	28.10	1180.20	48.97			
DRIVER OVERNIGHT	1.17	48.97	1.17			
PARKING LHC - 10 DAYS	5.43	250.00	5.43			
TOTALS	2164.89	99335.11	2906.63	2098.89	2039.30	1489.30
FARE PER PERSON w/2nd overnight	**2525.00**	116150.00	**3266.00**	**2459.00**	**2399.00**	**1849.00**
PROJECTED NET PROFIT	360.11	**16814.89**	359.37	360.11	359.70	359.70

226

Figure 31 – Customer Invoice for a "major" tour to New England.

TOUR INVOICE

BARTLETT TOURS
4065 Northstar Drive
Lake Havasu City, AZ 86406
928 680-4142

INVOICE DATE: 07/19/2010

TOUR NAME:

BACK ROADS OF NEW ENGLAND
October 10-18, 2010

TRAVELERS:

JOHN & JANE DOE

The first and last names shown to the left MUST
match the names shown on your drivers license
for airport check-in. Call if there is a difference.

# TRAVELERS	DESCRIPTION	PER PERSON	AMOUNT
2	Tour Package from Lake Havasu City	2,495.00	4,990.00
2	Return Overnight in Las Vegas*	30.00	60.00
		SUBTOTAL	5,050.00
*Originally estimated at $65 per person.		LESS: DEPOSIT	(500.00)
		BALANCE DUE	**$4,550.00**

Please retain this invoice for your records

Sorry, we don't accept credit cards

Please pay before August 10, 2010

Make all checks payable to Bartlett Tours

The above tour package includes roundtrip bus transportation from Lake Havasu City to Las Vegas, overnight in
Las Vegas with group buffet dinner, 1 light dinner on arrival in Boston hotel and the complete tour package as
described in the detailed itinerary. Gratuities for guides and drivers are not included.

Insurance to cover trip cancellation and interruption, trip delay, uninsured medical expense, emergency evacuation and
baggage protection is available through Travel Guard. If you have not purchased travel insurance, you may still do so.
However, insurance purchased more than 15 days after date of tour deposit will not cover claims resulting from any
pre-existing medical conditions.

Cancellation Charges for this tour: Deposits were non-refundable after May 10, 2010. From August 11 until 16 days prior
to departure, cancellation fee is 20% of total tour price; 15-1 days prior to departure, cancellation fee is 40% of total price;
day of departure and after, cancellation fee is 100% of total price. If cancellation is necessary, and you purchased travel
insurance, you must seek reimbursement through a claim with Travel Guard .

THANK YOU FOR TRAVELING WITH BARTLETT TOURS

Figure 32 – Customer "important information" for our New England tour.

BARTLETT TOURS
Back Roads of New England - 2010

IMPORTANT INFORMATION
(Please read now and then again before we leave)

Air Tickets: We will have your air tickets and tour documents and will pass them out on the motorcoach on the way to Las Vegas.

Correct Names: Please be certain that your first and last names on the enclosed invoice match the identification that you will be using. If we are showing a nickname rather than your given name (i.e. Betty rather than Elizabeth) please call now so that we can make the change before ordering your air tickets. The names on the tickets must match your picture ID (driver's license). You will be required to present ID when checking in for our flights.

To Las Vegas: We will leave promptly at **2:00pm, Sunday, October 10** from our regular parking lot on Swanson Avenue, behind the Lake Place Inn. You may leave your car in the locked and fenced lot while we are gone. Our overnight will be at the Fiesta Henderson with a group buffet dinner included. We will depart at 6:45am sharp Monday to allow plenty of time for group check-in and breakfast at the airport on your own.

Our Flights: (all on American Airlines)
Monday, Oct 11
#582 - Las Vegas to Chicago O'Hare	Depart 9:55am	Arrive 3:30pm
#154 - Chicago to Boston Logan	Depart 5:15pm	Arrive 8:25pm

Monday, Oct 18
#1099 - Boston to Dallas Ft Worth	Depart 3:45pm	Arrive 7:00pm
#1595 - Dallas to Las Vegas	Depart 7:50pm	Arrive 8:40pm

As you are probably aware, there will be no meal service on our flights. However, American Airlines does offer the opportunity to purchase breakfast, lunch and dinner items depending on the time of day. You must pay by credit card - no cash. You are also allowed to bring onboard food and drinks purchased inside the security gates of the airport.

Charge for Checked Bag: Each person on the tour is allowed one large piece of luggage. American Airlines has a $25 charge for one checked bag per person, measuring 62 inches or less when you add the height, width and length. The weight limit is 50 pounds. If the bag weighs over 50 pounds, there is an additional $50 charge. These charges must be paid at check-in using a credit card.

Pack Overnight Items: Because of the need for an early departure for the Las Vegas airport, we will leave the large bags on the bus overnight in Las Vegas. Please pack sleep wear, necessary toiletries and a change of clothes, if desired, in your carryon bag. This will expedite our departure from the hotel at 6:45am on Monday morning. A carryon must not exceed **45 inches** when you total length plus width plus height. Remember not to pack any liquids in containers larger than 3 oz in your carryon (see enclosed "Helpful Tips for Air Travel").

Our Hotel in Boston: DoubleTree Guest Suites Boston,
400 Soldiers Field Road, Boston, MA
617 783-0090

Late and Light Dinner: Since the group arrival at the hotel will be approximately 9:30-10:00, we have made arrangements for a carving station serving baked Virginia ham, with macaroni and cheese, glazed carrots and buttermilk biscuits to be open in a banquet room from 9:30 - 10:30pm. Our Collette Tour Manager will be there for us to meet before we head off to bed.

At Tours End: On Monday, October 18 we will leave Boothbay Harbor, Maine for a beautiful drive along the shoreline through Kenebunkport to Boston with arrival at the airport in the early afternoon. We'll have time for check-in for our **3:45pm flight** and lunch at the airport. We will change planes in Dallas and continue on to Las Vegas. Our flight is scheduled to arrive in Las Vegas at 8:40pm with estimated bus departure with all of us and our luggage at about 9:30pm (12:30am Boston time).

Return to Lake Havasu City: Due to our late arrival, a long day of travel and a 3-hour time change, we have decided we will all be ready for some sleep. We have hotel reservations at the Fiesta Henderson with breakfast the next morning before continuing to Lake Havasu. (The note at the bottom of the Detailed Itinerary warned that this might be necessary and that the additional cost would be $65 per person. Due to favorable charter bus and hotel rates, we were able to get the figure down to $30 per person - $50 for a single room, which is shown on your tour invoice). Our bus will depart at 9:00am Tuesday morning with expected arrival back in Lake Havasu at 1:00pm (after losing one hour coming back into Arizona).

What to Pack: Weather in New England in October will be typical fall weather with likely highs in the 50's and low 60's and lows in the 30's and 40's. Dressing in layers is the best plan, but be sure to bring a warm jacket. Dress for all of the tour will be casual to dressy casual. Bring something for the possibility of rain.

Luggage: <u>Only one</u> checked bag per person, and no garment bags please. Make sure your luggage has <u>your</u> name, address and phone number on the outside AND the inside before leaving home. You will be given a luggage tag at the bus to attach to each checked bag to identify it as part of our group. In addition, you may bring a small carryon bag that you'll take on the bus and plane with you. Please put a colorful pompom or ribbon on your large bag so you can spot it when we ask you to verify the presence of your bag in our group of bags at baggage claim. You <u>will not</u> handle your bags when we arrive at our final destination airports, but we want you to verify that your bag is there before the Sky Caps move them all to the bus.

Collette Carryon Bag: As a gift from Collette, each of you will receive a green, canvas bag that is suitable for use as a carryon. I will notify you when the bags have arrived and you can pick them up at our home. You are not required to use these bags on our tour! If you have something you like better, please bring it.

Emergency Phone Numbers:
Fiesta Henderson, Henderson, NV   702 558-7000
Gordon's cell phone (only while on tour)   928 210-xxxx

Other Questions? If you have other questions, please feel free to call us at 928 680-xxxx.

BARTLETT TOURS

Helpful Tips for Domestic Air Travel

Since some of you may not have traveled by air since new security regulations have gone into effect, we wanted to provide some tips to make your check-in quick and comfortable.

Do not leave your bags unattended in the airport for any reason. When traveling in a group, ask someone else to stay with your bags when you need to use the restroom or leave for a short time.

Do not expect any meals on today's airlines. Feel free to carry your own snack bars, candy, trail mix, etc. on the flights. Delta <u>will</u> offer meals for sale on board, but take some snacks just in case.

CARRY-ON LUGGAGE

- Carry-on luggage is limited to one small carry-on bag plus one personal item such as a purse or camera case.
- Put all undeveloped film and cameras with film in your carry-on baggage. The X-Ray equipment used for carry-on bags will not damage your film. It should not be put into your checked bags.
- Carry prescription medications in your carry-on bag. Insulin users can carry a reasonable supply of syringes along with other supplies with pharmacy labels to identify them as such.
- No sharp items can be carried with you onto the plane, either in pockets, purse or carry-on.

Prohibited items in your carry-on bag include:
- Weapons of any kind
- Pocket knives of any size
- Scissors with sharp pointed tips
- Any item with a blade, such as box cutters, utility knives, etc.
- Tools, such as screwdrivers, pliers, wrenches, etc.
- Cigarette lighters, strike-anywhere matches or lighter fluid
- Mace or Pepper Spray
- Liquids, gels, lotions or aerosols in larger than 3 oz containers (OK in checked luggage)

If found, these items will be confiscated at the carry-on bag inspection point. If you want to take some of these items, such as scissors or a pocket knife, they can be packed in your checked luggage.

The "3-1-1" Rule for Carry-on Bags

3 All liquids, gels, lotions or aerosols must be in containers of **3 oz or less**.
If the container is 6 oz yet is only half full, it will still be confiscated)

1 All 3 oz or smaller containers must be in a **ONE QUART**-size, clear zip-lock bag.

1 You are allowed just **ONE** zip-lock bag per passenger
(no exceptions - use a <u>single</u> QUART size bag, not a gallon bag or anything else)

This clear zip-lock bag must be taken out of your carry-on and run through the X-Ray machine
on top of the bin with your shoes, coat, keys, etc.

(over)

CHECKED LUGGAGE

- Be sure you have your name and address on the outside (with a tag) and on the inside of your checked bags. If the tag should get pulled off, your name and address will still be inside.

- <u>Do not lock your suitcase</u>. Inspection of checked bags will generally be done in the back rooms after you have checked in and left for the gate. If inspectors determine the need to randomly search your bag, they will need to break the lock and will not be responsible for the damage. If your bag was purchased in the last 4-5 years, it may have a key-lock marked "TSA". If so, then you are allowed to lock your bag, since TSA can unlock it without breaking anything.

- If inspectors do search your checked luggage, an official TSA note will be left inside your bag indicating that it has been opened and searched.

- Don't overload your luggage. If opened, it will be more difficult for the inspector to repack.

- Delta Airlines checked luggage charges from delta.com are as follows:

  "First bag free; second bag, $25. There will be a $5 surcharge on the second checked bag when checking in via ticket counter, kiosk, or curbside. There is no surcharge for bags prepaid during online check-in at delta.com".

  Bags over 50 lbs will incur a charge of $90.

Passing Through the Security Checkpoint

Passing through security is easy and simple if you just follow the rules.

- You will need to show your boarding pass and passport as you get in the line.

- Usually, you will need to show your boarding pass again to the attendant as you walk through the metal detector.

- Take off your hat, shoes and coat and put them in a bin to go through the X-Ray.

- Remove the single, one-quart zip-lock bag with your liquids and place it on top of the bin.

- If you have a Camcorder or Cell phone, put it in the bin for X-Ray.

- If you have a pace-maker or a metal hip or knee, just tell the person at the X-Ray unit and they will take you around the metal detector and use a hand wand to check you.

- If your carry-on is singled out for a more detailed check, it is usually a random thing. Don't be offended or ask the attendant why you were chosen. Just let him do his job and it will be quicker.

- Once through the metal detector, make sure you collect all your items from the X-Ray belt, then move to a point out of the way to put on your shoes and repack any other items.

Knowing the rules and playing by the rules makes the process easier and almost pleasant.

Figure 34– Driver Itinerary for an airport transfer to Las Vegas.

BARTLETT TOURS

4065 Northstar Drive
Lake Havasu City, AZ 86406

2010 New England Tour - Itinerary for Ryans Express

Sunday, October 10, 2010

	AM	Deadhead to Lake Havasu City
		Lake Place Inn - fenced parking lot in 2000 block of Swanson Ave
	1:15p	Spot bus at parking lot - gate will be open at 1:00pm
	2:00	Depart Lake Havasu for Henderson
2:00	3:45	Lake Havasu City to Searchlight
3:45	4:05	Rest Stop at Terrible's Truck Stop
4:05	5:00	Searchlight to Fiesta Henderson
6:00	7:30	Dinner at Fiesta Buffet

Driver to stay overnight at the Fiesta due to our early departure Friday am.
Room and dinner provided by Bartlett Tours.
Large bags to stay overnight on bus

Monday, October 11

	6:25a	Spot bus at Fiesta Henderson Main entrance at back (circle)
6:45	7:05	Fiesta Hotel to McCarran Airport - American Airlines
		American Airlines Flight #582 departs at 9:55am

RETURN TRIP

Monday, October 18

	8:30p	Spot bus at McCarran Airport arrivals
	8:40p	Scheduled arrival of American Airlines flight #1595 (2040 hours)
9:00	9:30	Load luggage and pax
9:30	9:45	McCarran Airport to Fiesta Henderson
9:45	10:00	Check-in and overnight

**Driver to stay overnight at the Fiesta to avoid keeping our guests up waiting for their
bags to be delivered. Large bags to stay overnight on bus.**
Room and breakfast to be provided by Bartlett Tours.

Tuesday, October 19

		Breakfast at Denny's inside Fiesta Hotel Casino - Coupons
	8:40	Spot bus at Main Entrance (circle)
9:00	9:55	Travel to Terrible's Truck Stop at Searchlight

9:55   10:15   Rest Stop at Terrible's Truck Stop
10:15   12:00   Searchlight to Lake Havasu City

DRIVER:

Note: You will be staying overnight with the group even though we are in Las Vegas. This is due to the fact that we are leaving the luggage on the bus overnight and have a 6:45am departure for McCarran Airport.

Coming into Lake Havasu City from the north on AZ 95, turn left on Swanson Ave (just past the highway bridge in town). Continue on Swanson through one signal and three stop signs until you see a sign "LAKE PLACE INN" on your left. The sign is in the fenced parking lot of the motel. Continue to the big gate opening onto Swanson. The gate will be open at 1:00pm.

Please park the bus inside the fenced lot where we will board. Back the bus parallel to the street into the end opposite the alley with the bus centered between the TWO AMBER REFLECTORS on the fence (you will be able to see the amber reflectors in your mirrors). Keep the rear of the bus about 8 feet from the fence. We'll load from that position.

You can call us at 928 680-xxxx or my cell phone, 928 210-xxxx.

Gordon Bartlett

Figure 35 – Example of a flyer for a "major" tour to Australia /New Zealand.

BARTLETT TOURS

presents...

AUSTRALIA & NEW ZEALAND
"South Pacific Wonders"

October 15-29, 2012

Let's go!

Explore two great countries of the Southern Hemisphere – Australia and New Zealand. From the tropical splendor of the Great Barrier Reef on Australia's northern coast, to the ethereal beauty of glacial fjords on New Zealand's South Island, this 15 day journey to the lands "down under" brings you the best of both countries at an enjoyable pace (3 nights in each hotel). Cruise Sydney Harbor and Milford Sound. Meet Australia's wildlife-up close. Discover the wonders of Aboriginal culture. Experience Queenstown, the adventure capital of the world.

Tour Highlights

Cairns, Great Barrier Reef, Sydney, Christchurch, Mount Cook National Park, Queenstown, Milford Sound

- Take in the sights during a delightful dinner cruise of Sydney Harbour.

- Enjoy a guided tour of the Sydney Opera House, an architectural wonder.

- Capture the amazing scenery of the fjords of New Zealand on a cruise of Milford Sound.

- Visit a Canterbury farmyard to see a sheep shearing demonstration and learn how this New Zealand family farm works.

$5,375 per person, dbl occupancy

$6,440 for a single room

Add $250 if booked after 4/15/12

Day 1: Monday, October 15, 2012
Depart From Home
We will depart from Lake Havasu City with some free time in Santa Monica before an evening arrival at LAX for our late flight to Cairns. Begin the adventure of a lifetime today! *Lunch included.*

Day 2: Tuesday, October 16
Travel Day
Due to the International Dateline we lose a full day now but we'll gain it back on our flight home.

Day 3: Wednesday, October 17
Arrive Cairns, Australia
Your tour begins today in Cairns, the gateway to the Great Barrier Reef. Don't forget to look up at the Southern Hemisphere's stars this evening after you join your mates for a welcome dinner. *Today dinner will be included.*

Day 4: Thursday, October 18
Cairns
Today visit the Tjapukai Aboriginal Cultural Center. You'll see traditional Aboriginal dances, learn about the Aboriginal lifestyle, and even throw a boomerang or play a didgeridoo, a traditional instrument. Browse the renowned art gallery and visit the interpretation center, which houses a collection of interesting artifacts. This afternoon a great experience awaits as you search for crocodiles in their natural

---

habitat during a visit to Hartley's Croc Farm! Boardwalks take you on a path of adventure through rainforests and woodlands to see animals such as wild birds, reptiles and wallabies. **While visiting you also have the chance to meet some of the local koalas and have a private talk with a wildlife naturalist to learn more about these cuddly creatures.** Then, enjoy an exciting cruise in the lagoon looking for crocodiles before enjoying a delicious Aussie barbecue. *Today breakfast and dinner will be included.*

Day 5: Friday, October 19
Great Barrier Reef
Board a high speed catamaran for an exciting excursion to the Great Barrier Reef.
This is an immense series of 2,800 coral reefs which are home to amazingly diverse marine life. From your base on Green Island, you are able to explore the reef in many ways. Enjoy a glass bottom boat ride*, a stroll on the walking trail to take in the rain forest, relax on the beaches, snorkel or just watch the fish and sea turtles swim past from the pier. For a more adventurous encounter with the reef, optional scuba diving and an outer reef tour are also available. Whichever way you choose, you'll see some of the world's most fascinating marine and plant life. *Today breakfast and lunch will be included.*

Day 6: Saturday, October 20
Cairns - Sydney
Your morning is at leisure for independent exploration. Later today, fly to the bustling city of Sydney. *Today breakfast will be included.*

234

Figure 35, continued.

Day 7: Sunday, October 21
Sydney
This morning enjoy a city tour of Sydney where the English explorer James Cook first weighed anchor in 1770. Highlights of your tour include Kings Cross, the Harbour Bridge, Chinatown, the Rocks, Circular Quay, the Botanic Gardens and the fashionable Paddington suburb. Then, discover one of the world's most fascinating architectural wonders during a guided tour of the Sydney Opera House. Next, enjoy a unique opportunity to learn first-hand how raw opals are transformed from the dark mine shafts to beautiful works of art. This evening is free to explore Sydney at your leisure. Maybe try one of Sydney's eclectic restaurants! *Today breakfast will be included.*

Day 8: Monday, October 22
Sydney
Enjoy a leisurely day to explore Sydney your way. Your Tour Manager will be on hand to offer suggestions. Tonight, experience the best of Sydney. **As you say your farewell to Australia, chat with new friends and take in the sights during a delightful dinner cruise of Sydney Harbour. The cruise takes in the beauty of Sydney's skyline and passes by Australia's two most famous icons: the renowned Sydney Opera House and the Harbour Bridge.** *Today breakfast and dinner will be included.*

Day 9: Tuesday, October 23
Sydney - Christchurch, New Zealand
You leave Australia behind and fly to New Zealand and the historic city of Christchurch. Upon arrival enjoy a short sightseeing tour of "the most English city outside of England." Highlights include magnificent gardens, the Neo-Gothic Cathedral and the downtown park district. *Today breakfast will be included.*

Day 10: Wednesday, October 24
Christchurch
This morning visit a Canterbury farmyard where you'll enjoy a sheep shearing demonstration and see the herding of the farm's animals! It's a great opportunity to learn how a New Zealand family farm operates. This afternoon you are free to explore Christchurch independently before a truly special evening. **Tonight you are the guest of honor at a private dinner inside the restored Riccarton House**

mansion. **Step back in time and experience a world of Victorian and Edwardian splendor during a guided tour that teaches you the history of the first family of Christchurch. Then, relax in the elegant dining room and enjoy a sumptuous dinner.** *Today breakfast and dinner will be included.*

Day 11: Thursday, October 25
Christchurch
Today, enjoy a day of exploration on your own in beautiful Christchurch. This English city — the charming international gateway to New Zealand's South Island — boasts countless cafes and boutiques. Stroll its cobblestone streets and enjoy the many sights that —the Garden City! has to offer. Make yourself right at home this evening when a New Zealand family welcomes you into their home for dinner! **This is sure to be an unforgettable evening during which you will make new friends, learn about the customs of the "Kiwi's" and enjoy a home-cooked meal.** *Today breakfast and dinner will be included.*

Day 12: Friday, October 26
Christchurch - Mt. Cook Region - Queenstown
Traverse the spectacular countryside to New Zealand's most famous national park, Mt. Cook. Mt. Cook is one of the most impressive mountains in the world with its jagged contours and nearly vertical slopes. You may choose to view the massive glaciers and extensive snow-covered mountain top terrain on an optional glacier flightseeing tour (weather permitting), or perhaps enjoy the park during a nature walk. Continue to Queenstown and enjoy a stop at a local fruit stand to gain an inside look at the produce of New Zealand. *Today breakfast will be included.*

Day 13: Saturday, October 27
Queenstown - Milford Sound - Queenstown
En route to Milford Sound, enjoy the rugged grandeur of the Hollyford Valley. You'll travel through beech forest via the Homer Tunnel. **During a cruise of the breathtakingly beautiful Milford Sound you'll see why this fjord is one of the most visited sites on the South Island. With rock faces that rise nearly 4,000 feet on either side, the scenery will take your breath away.** Following your cruise, you return to Queenstown. You may choose to

return via a short optional flight (weather permitting) for spectacular views of New Zealand's Southern Alps. *Today breakfast and lunch will be included.*

Day 14: Sunday, October 28
Queenstown
A leisurely day in Queenstown offers several options to enhance your vacation. Shop or people watch in the village or perhaps take the optional "Journey through Middle Earth" tour, which takes you through the majestic Remarkable Mountains and the breathtaking Queenstown countryside showcasing many of the spots where the Lord of the Rings movies were filmed. **This evening, take in the city of Queenstown from above and soak in the breathtaking views during a gondola ride to dinner at the Skyline Restaurant overlooking Queenstown, Lake Wakatipu and the mountains.** *Today breakfast and dinner will be included.*

Day 15: Monday, October 29
Queenstown - Tour Ends
Our flight passes the International Dateline and we gain the day back. We will land in Los Angeles in the morning and will head back to Lake Havasu. *Today breakfast will be included in Queenstown and breakfast or lunch will be included after landing at LAX.*

This tour will be conducted by **Collette Vacations** and a tour manager will be with us throughout our tour of both countries.

Included Features
12 nights accommodations
12 breakfasts, 4 lunches, 6 dinners
Professional tour manager
Baggage handling from hotel to hotel

Our Itinerary

Day 1-2	Overnight Flight
Day 3-5	Cairns
Day 6-8	Sydney
Day 9-11	Christchurch
Day 12-14	Queenstown
Day 15	Overnight Flight

A valid passport and the purchase of travel Insurance is required for this tour.

Figure 36 – Example of a flyer sent by mail or email to those inquiring about this cruise.

Pacific Coastal Cruise
April 28-May 5, 2012
7 Nights on Princess Cruise Lines'
"SAPPHIRE PRINCESS"

From Los Angeles to Los Angeles with exciting Ports of Call at
Santa Barbara, San Francisco, San Diego and Ensenada, Mexico

Prices below are per person, double occupancy and include the 7-night cruise, all meals and entertainment on board, port charges and taxes, round trip bus transportation to San Pedro Cruise Terminal, locked parking for your car in Lake Havasu, buffet lunch each way, and all tips for baggage handling.
Shore excursions, onboard gratuities and any future fuel surcharges are not included.

AVAILABLE STATEROOMS

			Per person Fare
Category BC	Balcony Stateroom	Deck 11	$1,595
Category EE (limited)	Outside Stateroom with Window	Deck 5	$1,435
Category J (limited)	Inside Stateroom (no window)	Deck 10	$1,195

Passport recommended, but US citizens taking "closed loop" cruises (US to US) are not required to have a passport but will need proof of citizenship such as an original or certified copy of a birth certificate, a certificate of naturalization or a passport card plus a drivers license or other government issued ID.

ITINERARY

		Arrive	Depart
April 28	Bus from Lake Havasu		8:00am
	Board ship and sail		4:00pm
April 29	Santa Barbara, California	7:00am	6:00pm
April 30	At Sea		
May 1	San Francisco	7:00am	10:00pm
May 2	At Sea		
May 3	San Diego	8:00am	6:00pm
May 4	Ensenada, Mexico	8:00am	5:00pm
May 5	San Pedro Pier	7:00am	
	Bus to Lake Havasu City	5:00pm	

Reserve now with $250 per person deposit
(Fully refundable up until final payment due February 6, 2012)

BARTLETT TOURS
928 680-4142

Figure 37 – Profit Projection of an ocean cruise, transfer to the LA pier only

BARTLETT TOURS - PROFIT PROJECTION OF MEXICAN RIVIERA CRUISE - JAN 9, 2011

TRANSFER TO & FROM LOS ANGELES PIER	PER PERSON	TOTAL	JOINING US
	51	51	AT PIER
ESTIMATED			
BUS CHARTER	90.59	4620.00	0.00
ROOMS FOR DRIVER (2 nights)	2.29	116.78	0.00
COFFEE & COOKIES	0.69	35.00	0.00
SNACK & WATER	0.49	25.00	0.00
SUNDAY DINNER AT HOME TOWN	12.50	637.50	0.00
TIP AT LUNCH	0.78	40.00	0.00
BAGGAGE HANDLING AT PIER in/out	4.00	204.00	0.00
BUS DRIVER TIPS	1.96	100.00	0.00
PARKING LHC	4.41	225.00	0.00
SUNDAY DINNER AT HOME TOWN	12.50	637.50	0.00
TIP AT LUNCH	0.78	40.00	0.00
ON-BOARD TIPS	3.92	200.00	3.92
TOTAL COST	134.92	6880.78	3.92
TRANSFER PER PASSENGER	275.00	14025.00	144.00
NET PROFIT BEFORE CRUISE	140.08	7144.22	140.08

(The net profit figure of $7144.22 will be used in the second spreadsheet which will add cruise commission)

Figure 38 - Total Profit Projection, including commissions, of an ocean cruise.

MEXICAN RIVIERA PACKAGE RATES - JAN 16, 2011

RCCL MARINER OF THE SEAS

CATEGORY	Balcony E2	Window I	Inside N	3RD PAX* ALL CATS
CRUISE ONLY	640.00	540.00	400.00	0.00
NCF*	159.00	159.00	159.00	159.00
PORT CHGS & TAX	56.54	56.54	56.54	56.54
TRANSFER PKG	275.00	275.00	275.00	275.00
PROFIT FACTOR	118.46	118.46	108.46	108.46
TOTAL PACKAGE	**1249.00**	**1149.00**	**999.00**	
SINGLE SUPPL 100%	640.00	540.00	400.00	
SINGLE RATE	**1889.00**	**1689.00**	**1399.00**	
COMMISSION PERCENT**	11.25%	11.25%	11.25%	
NUMBER OF PAX	44	5	2	51
COMMISSION	3168.00	303.75	90.00	3561.75
OVERAGE ON TRANSFER				7144.22
PROFIT FACTOR	5212.24	592.30	216.92	6021.46
ESTIMATED PROFIT				**16727.43**

*NCF = Non-Commissionable Funds (extra profit for the cruise line)

** Total commission to the Agency was 15%. My portion was 75% of total commission, or 11.25%; the Agency kept 25% or 3.75%.

Figure 39 – *Profit Projection of our Erie Canal cruise in June, 2004.*

BARTLETT TOURS - ACCL ERIE CANAL CRUISE JUNE, 2004 EC04

	PER PERSON	TOTAL	SINGLE	MEET IN RHODE ISL
ACCL - 13 DAYS Warren to Warren				
	30	30	1	8
BUS CHARTER from Arrow	56.80	1704.00	56.80	
BUS DRIVER TIPS (2 TRIPS)	3.33	100.00	3.33	
DRIVER OVERNIGHT LHC	1.56	46.71	1.56	
COOKIES & COFFEE	0.83	25.00	0.83	
ALL SNACKS & WATER	0.50	15.00	0.50	
DINNER FIESTA INN	21.00	630.00	21.00	
HOTEL FIESTA INN	33.06	991.80	66.12	
PORTERAGE	5.00	150.00	5.00	
BREAKFAST FIESTA INN	8.00	240.00	8.00	
BUS TO AIRPORT	9.97	299.00	9.97	
DRIVER TIP	1.00	30.00	1.00	
SKYCAP TIPS PHX (OUT & IN)	2.00	60.00	2.00	
CONWAY BUS TRANSFERS	30.00	900.00	30.00	20.00
OVERNIGHT JOHNSON & WALES ARR	49.37	1480.95	98.73	49.37
DINNER J&W	26.00	780.00	26.00	26.00
BREAKFAST J&W	12.00	360.00	12.00	12.00
HOTEL JOHNSON & WALES DEPART	40.04	1201.20	80.08	40.04
DINNER J&W	22.00	660.00	22.00	22.00
BREAKFAST J&W (Comp Contl)	0.00	0.00	0.00	0.00
LUNCH J&W	16.00	480.00	16.00	16.00
PORTERAGE J&W ($2 r/t)	4.00	120.00	4.00	4.00
BUS AIRPORT TO FIESTA INN	9.97	299.00	9.97	
DINNER AT FIESTA INN	21.00	630.00	21.00	
OVERNIGHT FIESTA INN	33.06	991.80	33.06	
BREAKFAST FIESTA INN	8.00	240.00	8.00	
PARKING LHC	14.17	425.00	14.17	
CRUISE FOR 2ND ESCORT - NET	0.00	0.00	0.00	
AIR FOR 2ND ESCORT + TAX 1ST ESC	9.90	297.00	9.90	9.90
TOTALS	438.55	13156.46	561.01	199.31

239

Figure 39 continued.

20'S CABINS	2086.75		3651.81	2086.75
PORT CHARGES	200.00		200.00	200.00
AIR PHX SW + AGENCY FEE	284.70		395.73	0.00
OPTIONAL EXCURSIONS	120.00		120.00	120.00
TRANSFER COST	438.55		561.01	199.31
TOTAL COST	3130.00		4928.55	2606.06
PRICE PER PASSENGER (20'S CABINS)	**3375.00**		**5174.00**	**2851.00**
NET PROFIT	245.00		245.00	245.00
40's CABINS	2375.75	71272.50	4751.50	2375.75
PORT CHARGES	200.00	6000.00	200.00	200.00
AIR PHX SW + AGENCY FEE	284.70	8541.00	284.70	0.00
OPTIONAL EXCURSIONS	120.00	3600.00	120.00	120.00
TRANSFER COST	438.55	13156.46	438.55	199.31
TOTAL COST	3419.00	102569.96	5794.75	2895.06
PRICE PER PASSENGER (40'S CABINS)	**3670.00**	110100.00	**6046.00**	**3146.00**
NET PROFIT	251.00	7530.04	251.00	251.00
50's CABINS	2537.25			2537.25
TOTAL COST	3580.50			3056.56
PRICE PER PASSENGER (50'S CABINS)	**3830.00**			**3306.00**
NET PROFIT	249.50			249.50
PROFIT BEFORE COMMISSION	249.50	7530.04		249.44
AVG COMMISSION 10%	245.65	7369.50		245.65
PROJECTED PROFIT	495.15	14899.54		495.10

Figure 40 – Screenshot of a blank page in Approach ready for a new travelers' info.

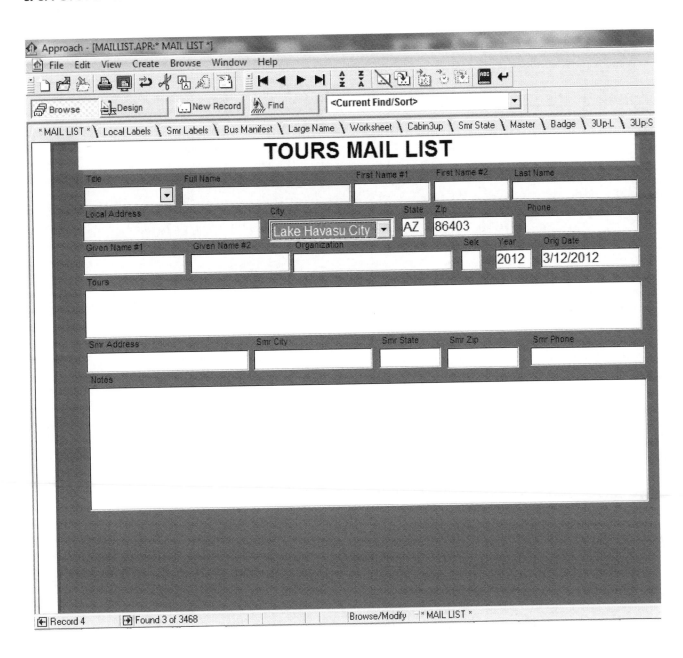

Figure 41 – Screenshot of the customer record of a frequent traveler (fictitious name).

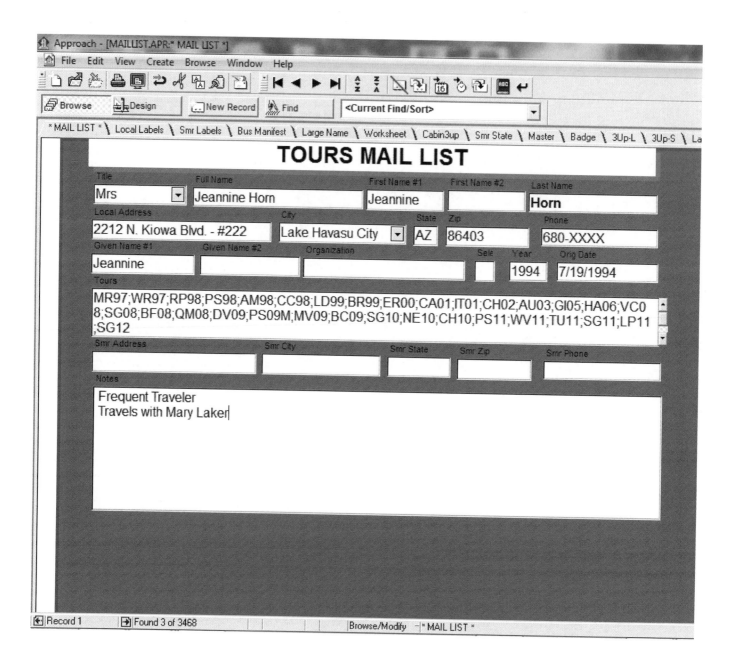

Figure 42 – An article I wrote for Groups Today magazine March/April 2010.

5 MINUTES WITH... **Gordon Bartlett**

Gordon Bartlett, owner of Bartlett Tours, talked with *Groups Today* about being a group travel planner in a remote location—and his formula for success.

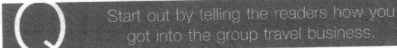

Start out by telling the readers how you got into the group travel business.

I retired from IBM in 1991, having always been in sales and marketing. I liked people, and I liked talking. My wife had some experience in Tucson helping her best friend start a senior citizens center at a local school district. That evolved to the point that they began taking their members on day trips in borrowed school vans, then overnights, then week-long tours around the Western states. My wife loved doing it and I thought that would be an exciting way to have a second career, since I was just 53 when I retired from IBM. We moved from Tucson to a place where we had vacationed for many years, Lake Havasu City, Arizona, and began Bartlett Tours. Our initial plan that we have stuck to is, 1) never have an employee, and 2) never own a bus. Patty and I have escorted 167 tours and cruises in nineteen years.

How have you managed to be successful even though you are in a remote location?

We have been successful with our tour company because we treat people with respect and we make sure they have plenty of laughs on our tours. Our tag line is "with Bartlett Tours, it's the experience." It's not just the destination that's important. It's not just the route or the scenery or the people you meet along the way that are important. Rather, it's the total experience of the travel that is the important thing. Being in a remote area, people are always looking for exciting things to do and interesting places to go. Our winter residents often say they want to see things in California, but they don't want to drive there. We provide one way for them to see California, and the world, in a safe, friendly way.

What is your strategy for creating group itineraries?

In coming up with new tours, we look for things that we think will be of general interest to the senior adults in our area. This has ranged from short overnight trips to Palm Springs or Phoenix for musical performances, to long tours to Australia, New Zealand and Fiji, Europe, China, Canada, Mexico, and Tahiti. Our clientele have come to know that they will be escorted by "Gordon and Patty" and they have confidence that we will provide an unforgettable "experience."

Are there lessons you've learned from operating in a remote location that can be useful to any group planner? What are they?

Whether operating in a remote location or a big city, I think the most important factor to the success of a tour is to have a good, well-planned itinerary. Once on the tour, no changes are made to the itinerary. As the tour director, I make all the decisions. We don't ever ask our groups to vote on anything. I explain to them, with a smile, that, "This tour is not a democracy—it is a benevolent dictatorship, and I'm the dictator." Before the tours, I check on everything—restaurant reservations, attractions, step-on guides, etc., so that we never have had a "forgotten" reservation. We tell our groups up front that we operate our tours on time and that when we ask them to be back on the bus at a certain time, we expect them to be in their seats, ready for the wheels to roll. We have an almost perfect on-time record, and our travelers very much appreciate it. G

243

Figure 43 – Sample of a Frequent Traveler Award

BARTLETT TOURS

FREQUENT TRAVELER AWARD

John & Jane Doe

As our way of saying "thank you" for your continued travel with us,
please enjoy lunch or dinner as our guest at either

Shugrue's, Barley Brothers or Javelina Cantina

Choice of Menu, tax and gratuity included.
Alcoholic beverages, lobster items, and dessert not included.

Please present this certificate to your server
This coupon does not expire, but please enjoy your meal soon.

BARTLETT TOURS

FREQUENT TRAVELER AWARD

Dora Smithers

As our way of saying "thank you" for your continued travel with us,
please enjoy lunch or dinner as our guest at either

Shugrue's, Barley Brothers or Javelina Cantina

Choice of Menu, tax and gratuity included.
Alcoholic beverages, lobster items, and dessert not included.

Please present this certificate to your server
This coupon does not expire, but please enjoy your meal soon.

Figure 44 - An 81/2 x 11 size card that I used inside the bus windshield

to identify our bus and tour company.

Color is bright yellow cardstock with red logo , then laminated.